AT THE HOUSE OF

THOMAS POYNTZ

The betrayal of William Tyndale with the

consequences for an English merchant and his family

Brian Buxton

Published by Brian Buxton 2013

ISBN 978-0-9926736-0-4

Cover illustration : Lofzangen ter eere Keizer Maximiliaan en zijn zoon Karel dern Vijfde. Met de Opitiis 1925 facsimile Woodcut of Antwerp 1515.

© The British Library Board (L.R.261.d.3 Woodcut of Antwerp 1515).

Printed by Lavenham Press,
47 Water Street, Lavenham, Suffolk CO10 9RN

Contents

'a poor man that has no promotion nor looks for none having no quality whereby he might obtain honour but of a very natural zeal and fear of God and his prince had liefer live a beggar all the days of his life and put himself in jeopardy to die rather than to live and see those leering curs to have their purpose'

Thomas Poyntz to his brother August 1535

PREFACE

The sayde Tyndall being in the towne of Andwarpe, was and hadde bene lodged about one whole yeare in the house of Thomas Pointz an Englisheman, who kept there an house of Englyshe marchauntes.

John Foxe Acts and Monuments

Around 1530 an Englishman, Thomas Poyntz, and his Flemish wife, Anna, were managing a lodging house for some of the English merchants based in Antwerp. They could hardly have imagined that this home would become the focal point of a plot to destroy arguably the most significant Englishman of the Reformation movement, William Tyndale, nor that from this house Poyntz would then mount a campaign aimed at saving Tyndale from martyrdom, an effort which was not only unsuccessful but which was to have dire personal consequences.

The family into which Thomas Poyntz was born held the manor of North Ockendon and other land in the south of Essex. It also had links with the city of London, in particular with the Goldsmiths' Company. Thomas himself was apprenticed and admitted to the Grocers' Company and seems to have set out on a career as a merchant trading between England and the Continent. In around 1526 he moved his base to Antwerp where he married a local woman, Anna van Calva, and in time they had four children. His life would seem to have been developing as one of reasonable prosperity and comfort, one which would have linked him with significant merchants and other London figures, but not a life he would have expected to involve him in high political or religious dramas.

His situation was to change for ever as a result of taking William Tyndale as a lodger in his house. Tyndale had left England shortly before Poyntz in order to pursue his ambition of translating the Bible into the English tongue from the original Greek and Hebrew, something nobody had attempted up to that time. By he arrived at the Poyntz household he had published the New Testament and had also produced sections of the Old Testament in English. In addition he had written a number of theological works which identified him with the reforming wing of the church, thus leading to his being marked as a heretic, at times his name being vilified in the same breath as that of Martin Luther.

Through the developing medium of printing his writings were being disseminated widely in England where, as across Europe, this was a time of religious turmoil. Also political and religious issues were often interwound.

Association with Tyndale, or possession of his writings, put a person in danger of interrogation, at least, and possibly much worse. It was hardly surprising that there were those who wanted to see him removed but that was less easy with someone living and travelling on the continent than with a home based heretic who could more easily be condemned to the fires of Smithfield. Attempts had been made to lure Tyndale back to England but he was deeply suspicious of such invitations and with good reason.

So it was that the house of Thomas Poyntz became of interest to a young Englishman, Henry Phillips, who was the means of placing Tyndale into the hands of the authorities in Brussels and who later engineered the imprisonment of Poyntz himself. Much mystery still surrounds this man and the scheming of which he was the public face.

As to Poyntz himself, through his association with William Tyndale and his sense of duty to this man when arrested, he became the most active in seeking Tyndale's freedom. As a result he placed himself in great danger. He was imprisoned but managed to flee back to England. Now separated from his family, seemingly for ever from his wife, unable to carry on his business, and in increasing debt, he suffered a kind of living martyrdom for almost twenty years. His is an extraordinary story of a man who, without any such intention, found himself caught up in the complex religious and political scene of his time.

Returning to the England of Henry VIII and appealing to the king for help when his sons were snatched from his control, receiving support from Edward VI, surviving the reign of Mary despite his Tyndalian past, Thomas Poyntz must have found some security in the last years of his life when he inherited the family estates in Essex.

He died in the fourth year of Queen Elizabeth's reign, now not in his own house but in that of a distant relative in London. Yet in Antwerp it had been his house which saw the dramatic events surrounding the taking of William Tyndale. Here Tyndale spent his last months of study, translation and writing. Here his downfall was cunningly engineered and from here he was encouraged out only to be promptly arrested. In his own house Poyntz then planned and talked and wrote, seeking in vain to free his former tenant from the otherwise inevitable burning, and very likely it was from this same house that he too was taken.

1. FORBEARS, FAMILY AND NEIGHBOURS

i. The Poyntz Family of Essex

And the aforesaid jurors say that the aforesaid manors and other premises are held of John, abbot of the monastery of St Peter, Westminster, by the right of his aforesaid monastery by fealty and the rent of £10 a year for all services and secular demands.

Inquisition Post Mortem on William Poyntz July 1527

Of the local gentry families that would have been known to the young William Tyndale growing up in Gloucestershire one would have been the Poyntz family settled at Acton Court in the village of Iron Acton. This notable local family was headed by Sir Robert Poyntz whose marriage to an illegitimate niece of Queen Elizabeth Wydeville had helped to raise his profile. His valour at the Battle of Bosworth and his loyalty to Henry VII brought favours and, in due course, appointments in the household of Henry VIII's first queen, Catherine of Aragon.

The family of Sir Robert was descended from the second marriage of a Nicholas Poyntz early in the fourteenth century. From this man's first marriage, to an Elizabeth de la Zouche, descended the lesser known Poyntz family of Essex.

It is not certain exactly when this family arrived at North Ockendon. A grandson of Nicholas, also named Nicholas, is sometimes described as of Tockington in Gloucestershire and sometimes of North Ockendon in Essex. It is only with his son, Poncius, that the Poyntz's presence is more clearly recorded and with this man's marriage the name became inextricably linked with that manor which the family of his wife, Eleanor, had previously held. [1]

This was a period when Essex, like most of England, was disturbed by the social and economic changes which followed the decimation of the population in the Black Death of 1349. Manorial lords found that it was increasingly difficult to enforce feudal obligations as the shortage of labour gave ordinary people some leverage in dealing with their masters and opened up new opportunities. The ensuing unrest culminated in the Peasants' Revolt of 1381 when many men from Essex were present at the face to face meetings in London between the rebels and the teenage king, Richard II. The communities of Fobbing and Brentwood, both within ten miles of North Ockendon, were centres of insurrection. Local gentry were physically attacked and many manorial records were destroyed. The more immediate local area was stirred up by two individuals in particular, one of whom, Wiliam Roger, came from the neighbouring parish of South Ockendon where Poncius and Eleanor held another manor. [2]

The paucity of surviving records for North Ockendon makes it impossible to be clear what attitude Poncius and Eleanor took to the developing situation. Some lords tried to enforce feudal obligations on their tenants, whilst others recognised that change was inevitable. For example, some began to negotiate an annual payment in lieu of labour obligations on the manorial estates. Certainly the feudal system in its strictest sense was breaking down.

The church of St. Mary Magdalene, North Ockendon, Essex. The chapel on the right contains the tombs and memorials of the Poyntz family. The tower was built in the fifteenth century, in part with legacies from the grandfather and great-grandfather of Thomas Poyntz.

The date of the marriage of Poncius and Eleanor is unknown but records show them active in the area by the mid 1370s. In 1393 Poncius exercised his right to present a priest to the parish, something the Poyntz family continued to do at alternate vacancies until 1526 when they acquired the sole right of presentation.[3]

The lands which now came into the Poyntz family lie some twenty miles east of the city of London and just north of the Thames. The manor of North Ockendon itself was held from the abbot of Westminster. William the Conqueror had given this manor to Westminster Abbey as part of an exchange for that of Windsor when he wished to build a castle to guard the western outskirts of London. [4]

The manor in South Ockendon which was a part of the inheritance of Eleanor became known as the Manor of Poyntz. For this estate some records do survive, including a copy of a manorial court session of 1391. [5]

Surviving wills, inquisitions post mortem and deeds dating from the fifteenth and sixteenth centuries show the Poyntz family as holding other land in several places within six miles of North Ockendon. This included, on higher gound to the north, around Brentwood, Childerditch, South Weald and Warley; to the east on the low lying 'fen' around Bulphan, Dunton and East Horndon; to the west around Upminster; and around Aveley and Grays Thurrock to the south.

How these various acreages became linked to the manor of North Ockendon is not always clear. Some were probably part of the inheritance of Eleanor whilst others may have been leased to meet specific needs. The higher land to the north was well wooded, as it is still today. There are references to marshland, probably by the Thames in Grays Thurrock which may have been used for grazing sheep, although there was also the fen district around Bulphan where streams flow down from the higher ground so leading to the name 'Seven Fountains' being found in manuscripts referring to this area. Sixteenth century records detail a thousand acres of land, presumably arable, five hundred acres of pasture, and forty acres of meadow for hay. [6]

At some early stage the family also acquired land south of the Thames, in Kent, but how this came about is not recorded and details of this holding are vague. The wills of John, son of Poncius, in 1447, and of his son, also John, in 1469, refer to a 'manor of East Wickham' but the Poyntz family certainly did not hold the manor of East Wickham, the ownership of which is clearly recorded. At the time of the sale in 1499 the 'manor' is described as being located in Bexley, Plumstead and Woolwich. Perhaps a number of pieces of land were collectively but informally described and operated as a manor.[7]

That North Ockendon was the business centre of the Poyntz estates is clear from the two fifteenth century wills. Both Johns described themselves as 'of North Ockendon' and both requested burial in the fourteenth century Lady Chapel of the parish church of St. Mary Magdalene, a chapel today filled with the memorials to successive generations of the family. No trace remains of the manor house in which they lived, nor of any of its successors, although a partially surviving moat indicates the site. The parish church stands only a few yards away. Like Poncius and Eleanor before them, the two Johns would have entered the church by the twelfth century south door. The rows of zig-zag and billet carving of its round arch will have caught their eye as it still does worshippers today. In the fifteenth century the building of the church was a work in progress. John, in 1447, left £10 towards the making of the bell-tower, whilst, in 1469, his son left 10 Marks towards 'the new work of the steeple'. This work is the tower which still stands today. The younger John also left 6s 8d for the glazing of the west window.

In view of the association his grandson was to have with William Tyndale it is interesting to note in the will of the younger John the traditional bequests to ensure the passage of his soul through purgatory, something which in the next century Tyndale was to come to vehemently attack. John left money for a priest to pray for his soul, the souls of his family and of the people of North Ockendon, for a year after his death. No doubt the priest would also serve wider needs of the parish. John's executors were to lay out 26s 8d for a stone slab over his grave as a reminder to parishioners that they should pray for him.

The will of this younger John refers to his having two sons. Thomas was the heir, whilst the younger, William, was to receive the manor of East Wickham in Kent for the duration of his life. Nothing more is known of Thomas. William began to work towards a career as a goldsmith, being apprenticed in 1477 to Edmund Shaa. Thomas must have died young as William, together with Edmund Shaa, presented a priest to North Ockendon in 1481. William was admitted to the livery of the Goldsmiths' Company in 1485. He is recorded as paying his quarterage, membership fee, to the company in 1486 and 1487 but not thereafter. References to him after 1487 simply describe him as 'gentleman'. It must be assumed that he had to give up the idea of a career as a goldsmith about this time to accept family responsibilities, his brother having died during the course of his apprenticeship. [8]

At some point he married Elizabeth Shaa, niece of his master Edmund. So now his background as a member of a well established Essex family of yeoman or lesser gentry came together with one of the city of London's most distinguished families of the period.

ii. The Family of Elizabeth Shaa

Buckingham Happy were England, would this gracious prince
Take on himself the sovereignty thereof:
But, sure, I fear, we shall ne'er win him to it.
Lord Mayor Marry, God forbid his grace should say us nay!

William Shakespeare Richard III Act 3 Scene 7

City workers sipping a cocktail on the mezzanine floor of London's Royal Exchange will notice a series of paintings visible around the walls. If they walk up to the rail at the edge of the bar, thus looking down to see the complete image, they will find that the paintings represent incidents in the history of the city of London as imagined by various nineteenth century artists. These were commissioned by the Gresham Committee for the walls of the third Royal Exchange after the central courtyard was roofed over in 1883. The topics chosen span the centuries from early trade with the Phoenicians to Queen Victoria opening the present building in 1844. Intended to provide a stunning panorama of London's history, to be seen by visitors on entrance to the courtyard, they are now, disappointingly, only visible at close quarters from the mezzanine level following the installation of exclusive shops, bars and restaurants in 2001.

Amongst these paintings is one by Sigismund Goetze (1866-1939) entitled *The Crown Offered to Richard III at Baynards Castle* (1898).

This image takes the viewer back to the tense period in the summer of 1483 following upon the unexpected death of Edward IV. After the young Edward V and his brother were taken to the Tower of London, never to be seen again, their uncle, Richard duke of Gloucester, set about his claim to the throne. If Gloucester was to succeed a necessity was to swing the loyalty of London away from the legitimate child king and to ensure that its influence and wealth backed him instead.

Based on Shakespeare's version of the events of 1483 in his play Richard III, itself owing much to the account by Sir Thomas More, the painting in the Royal Exchange shows the imagined scene in Baynards Castle, Blackfriars, as

St. Mark's Church, Dukinfield, Cheshire, millennium window. This panel depicts Sir Edmund Shaa offering the homage of the City of London to King Richard III.

© St. Mark's Dukinfield Parochial Church Council

the mayor of London offers the homage of the city to Richard. Two bishops stand on the staircase viewing the scene, one seems to be watching warily as a crowd of soldiers acclaim Richard whilst the other has his eyes set on the mayor as if to warn him to be careful to offer his homage as previously agreed. The Duke of Buckingham leans against a pillar, smiling with satisfaction that the mayor is saying the right words. Richard looks in the distance, seeking to give the impression that he will be a reluctant king. The mayor kneels before him, attended by the sheriffs and aldermen of the city, pleading with the duke to accept the crown. [9]

There is much uncertainty as to how far the mayor delivered the allegiance of London willingly or under duress. Interestingly in his will he sought prayers for the soul of Edward IV but made no mention of Richard III. What is known for certain is his identity. He was Sir Edmund Shaa, master of William Poyntz and uncle of Elizabeth.

Edmund Shaa is chiefly remembered for this involvement in the accession crisis of 1483. It seems that he had a brother, Ralph, a priest and canon of St. Paul's, who was was persuaded to preach at Paul's Cross, an outdoor preaching station at the south east corner of St. Paul's Churchyard. Like many others who spoke to Londoners at this place over the centuries Ralph was called upon to swing the citizenry to the official line. In this case he was to explain that the marriage of Edward IV to his Queen, Elizabeth Wydeville, was void as the king had a previous nuptial contract and consequently that the young Edward V and his brother were illegitimate. Thus Ralph prepared the way for Edmund to call upon Londoners to acclaim Richard as king. Ralph died soon afterwards, some said in shame at what he had done. He had been a popular preacher but this sermon turned many against him.

Of course, there was much more to Edmund's life than the events of 1483. As a young man he had arrived in London from Dukinfield in Cheshire and obtained apprenticeship in the Goldsmiths' Company. At that time the livery companies of the city of London still served their traditional functions, including overseeing their craft by supervising apprenticeships and exercising quality control over goods produced by their members. The Goldsmiths' Company was responsible, as it is still today, for testing the quality of gold and silver and providing a hallmark – a mark stamped on an article at Goldsmiths' Hall. This requirement came into operation during Edmund Shaa's time with the Company. Also, since the thirteenth century the company had tested the coinage of the realm each year, a responsibility still exercised annually in the Trial of the Pyx. Whilst most livery companies are now essentially social and charitable bodies the Goldsmiths have retained a strong responsibility for the craft. Edmund Shaa would still feel at home in the present day Goldsmiths' Hall which stands in Foster Lane, on the same site as the hall frequented by he and his contemporaries.

Thus the young Edmund came under the surveillance of a company with which he would be associated throughout his life and which he would head as prime warden in 1476. A working goldsmith, he became engraver of the Tower Mint in 1462 and is recorded as making several loans to Edward IV.

After the crisis over the succession in 1483 he performed, as mayor, the customary function of offering wine and water to both Richard and his queen at the coronation banquet and retained the gold cups and ewers 'pursuant to the privileges, liberties, and customs of the city of London on such occasions'.

He managed to retain favour when Richard was killed at Bosworth in 1485 and the first Tudor, Henry VII, succeeded.

He died in 1488 and was buried in the Church of St Thomas of Acre in Cheapside, on the site of the birthplace of Thomas Becket and where today stands the hall of the Mercers' Company.

Bequests in Edmund's will included one to found a school in his home area of Stockport and so he is claimed as founder of Stockport Grammar School. London was still a walled city at this time and he left money to rebuild one of the city gates, Cripplegate, which stood at the top of his own street, Wood Street. No doubt those who lived around the gates would value them for security at night and so would appreciate them being kept in good order. In addition he left money to repair country roads in Essex, both around Horndon on the Hill where he held two manors, Arden Hall and Horndon House, and in Aveley. Bequests towards improving infrastructure in town and country were common in this period.[10]

Both Horndon and Aveley lie only a few miles from the home of the Poyntz family at North Ockendon. William Poyntz was one of three apprentices enrolled by Edmund Shaa at Goldsmiths' Hall in 1477. During his eight years at Shaa's home he must have had a close up view of the dramatic events of the summer of 1483 and here he met his master's niece, Elizabeth Shaa.

The parentage of Elizabeth is unclear. The eighteenth century historian John Strype, in his revision of John Stow's earlier history of London, described her brother John as the son of John Shaa of Rochford, a statement repeated later in the century by the historian of Essex, Philip Morant. Neither of these gave any source for this information and there seems nothing else recorded about the man. On the other hand, Elizabeth's brother in his will, refers to his manor at Stambridge in Rochford Hundred and documents in the Essex Record Office show members of the Shaa family in dispute over this manor in the mid-sixteenth century. Perhaps there is truth in the tradition picked up by Stow and Morant. [11]

It may be that their father died when Elizabeth and her brother were still young as they both seem to have had close ties with their uncle. This is shown in the matters of Elizabeth's marriage and John's request to be buried by his uncle.

It was quite usual at this period to find masters arranging the marriage of an apprentice to a member of their family. Obviously the long apprenticeship gave good opportunity to observe the young men. An apprentice who came to be held in high regard by the master might well be considered a suitable person to marry a daughter of the house, or other relation, and maybe become heir to the business. At some point Edmund Shaa looked favourably upon William Poyntz and arranged a marriage for him with his niece Elizabeth.

William's new brother-in-law, John, followed in the steps of Sir Edmund in several respects. In 1482 Edmund made over to him the post of engraver of the Tower Mint. In addition John later became joint master of the Mint. In due time he served as a member of Parliament for the city of London, became the prime warden of the Goldsmiths' Company, was elected as an alderman and sheriff and, in 1501, mayor of London. In this last capacity he represented the city at the splendid festivities which surrounded the marriage of Prince Arthur to Catherine of Aragon at Old St. Paul's. According to the contemporary chronicler Robert Fabyan it was the habit of John Shaa as mayor to sit alone on many afternoon hearing and giving judgement on causes that were brought before him. Whilst popular with the poor this Court of Requests was not so with some lawyers because they saw Shaa as interfering in their sphere of work and no doubt losing them fees. Fabyan wrote that 'he favoured more sometime than justice and law required'. [12]

Following the death of Sir Edmund's widow, Dame Julian Shaa, in 1494, John received, by special act of Parliament, the right to inherit the Shaa lands, including the manors at Horndon on the Hill. He died in 1503. His sister slightly pre-deceased him but In his will he remembered William Poyntz whom he described as 'my brother'.

Through the Shaa connection the Poyntz family was very slightly related to Anne Brown, a step-daughter and niece by marriage of William Blount, fourth Baron Mountjoy (d1534). Mountjoy was a major patron of Desiderius Erasmus, the great Dutch scholar whose Greek text of the New Testament was to be the basis for Tyndale's translation. It was Mountjoy who first brought Erasmus to England in 1499 and subsequently gave him friendship and financial aid. Erasmus described Mountjoy as my 'continuing and most faithful Maecenas' (Maecenas having been a Roman statesman and patron of poets).

Anne first married (c1520) Mountjoy's nephew, John Tyrell, the son of his sister Constance, who lived at Heron Hall, Herongate only a few miles from the Poyntz family. Whether Mountjoy visited Herongate or knew the Poyntz family is unknown. There is record of his having adjudicated to sort out matters between his sister and nephew relating to various Essex lands and personal possessions after the death of his brother-in-law, Thomas Tyrell. To Anne he gave a book of hours which had belonged to her parents and which he dedicated to 'My nowne goode doghter and also nece ..... For wyth me yow be and shal Duryng my Lyue be yow asuryd Yore vertu hath me so well luryd'. [13]

Later Anne was to marry William Petre of Ingatestone (1542). Again she was not far from North Ockendon, no more than about twelve miles. She was now the wife of a significant figure of the Tudor court who served under Henry VIII, Edward, Mary and Elizabeth. She appears to have been on friendly terms with Princess Mary who visited her after the birth of her son John, later the first Baron Petre of Writtle. In the summer of 1553, Mary stayed overnight at Ingatestone during her accession progress from Framlingham to London and in September Anne rode in the coronation procession. The descendents of William and Anne still live in the house Sir William built at Ingatestone. [14]

iii. The Children of William and Elizabeth

They had as children John, Thomas, Henry and others.

Memorial tablet in North Ockendon church

On the brass memorial to William and Elizabeth in the church of St. Mary Magdalene, North Ockendon, there are shown six sons and six daughters but no names are given. Assuming that this indicates twelve children of the marriage then several have passed into total oblivion.

John appears to have been the eldest son, presumably named after his grandfather, followed by Thomas, probably named after the uncle he would never have known. There is evidence of at least two other sons. Edmund, probably named after Sir Edmund Shaa and seemingly with some interests in the Isle of Sheppey who had a daughter named Frideswide, and Henry who is named on a later memorial to William and Elizabeth in the church. In addition there is record of a William Poyntz being admitted to the Mercers' Company in 1517 who could well be another son. This leaves one son unremembered. [15]

Of the girls only two can be accounted for, Margaret and Julian. Margaret is mentioned in the will of her brother John in 1547 as Margaret Barley with a daughter Jane. Julian does not appear in any Poyntz family document but she is identified by two inscriptions each relating to one of her marriages.

First she married Henry Patmore of Much Hadham in Hertfordshire, 'citizen

Church of St. Andrew and cottages, Much Hadham, Hertordshire. Adjacent to the church was a residence of the bishops of London. A son of Henry Patmore by his first marriage was vicar.

and draper of London', as his second wife. Her father, William, was a feoffee, a kind of trustee, of the Essex lands of Henry and also an executor of the his will. He died in 1520 and was buried in St. Peter's, Cornhill, in the city of London where, according to John Stow, sixteenth century historian of London, there was a memorial which identified Julian as 'Julianæ filiæ Wilhelmi Poines de Essex', daughter of William Poyntz of Essex. [16]

In view of her brother Thomas' later association with William Tyndale, it is interesting to note that a son of Henry who was in trouble with the authorities for possession of forbidden religious books in 1530 may have been a son by the marriage to Julian. [17]

Julian's second husband came from a more distant part of the country, Cheshire. He was Sir Piers Dutton, a significant figure in that area. With him Julian worked on the building of an extension at their family home, Dutton Hall. Included in an eighty foot inscription carved just below the ceiling of the great hall are the words '... this hall and all the newe chambs .. were made and finished anno mccccxxxix bi the especiall devising of sr piers dutton knight and dame julian his wiff doghter of william ponies of northok'gtton in essex'. In c1930 the hall was dismantled and moved to Sussex where it still stands with the inscription intact.

Elizabeth Poyntz died in 1502, probably relatively young. William lived on until 1527, seemingly not re-marrying, when he died on the 21st January. He was succeeded by his son, John. [18]

It would appear that John did not marry until shortly after taking over the family estates. Although the exact date is unknown he was certainly married by 1532. His wife, Anne, may have brought or cemented important links with the notable families of Kent. [19]

For Anne this was a second marriage. On a memorial at North Ockendon she is described as sister and heir of Isaac Sibley of Buckinghamshire. However she was also the widow of John Cheyney of Sittingbourne in Kent who had died in 1527 leaving Anne and a daughter. [20]

 Although little is known about John Cheyney himself it seems clear from his will that he was at least associated with, and probably a relation of, Sir Thomas Cheyney who lived at Minster on the Isle of Sheppey and whose tomb can be seen there in the abbey church of the Blessed Virgin Mary and Saint Sexburgha. Sir Thomas was treasurer of the royal household and served the Tudor monarchy in various roles from boyhood, when he was a page in Henry VII's court, until his death early in the reign of Elizabeth. As a man of significance he would no doubt have had close contact with other Kent families who had a part to play in the unfolding dramas of the Tudor court, not least the Boleyns at Hever and and the Wyatts at Allington. Thomas Wyatt the Younger accompanied Thomas Cheyney on diplomatic missions but was also a poet of distinction. [21]

Surviving records from 1536 until his death in 1547 show John as performing the roles expected of a man of his standing at that period when there was no local government as we know it. Amongst his duties he was several times called upon to be a commissioner of the peace, one of those responsible for the administration of justice in the neighbourhood, also a commissioner of sewers with a duty to ensure against flooding, and, in 1546, a commissioner for the Six Articles which were aimed at enforcing a conservative religious policy on England. As 'John Poyntz of South Ukkingtom' he was summoned to the reception of Anne of Cleves on her arrival in England in December 1539.

By John's will his widow was to be his heir for the duration of her life before his lands descended through his brother Thomas. Thus manorial courts in her name are recorded at South Ockendon and she exercised her right to present a priest to the church at North Ockendon in 1554.

In the account of Queen Mary's coronation procession from the Tower to Westminster on 30th September 1553 Anne is described as 'mother of the maids' and it is clear from her will that she was serving at court at the time of her death. How this situation came about is uncertain. There are records of John and Anne sending gifts to Mary when she often lived in Essex as a princess. Possibly friendship with Anne Petre, second wife of Sir William Petre and a friend of Queen Mary, may be the explanation. As noted previously, Anne Petre was a distant relation and living at Ingatestone she was a near neighbour of the Poyntz family and was the same Anne who had earlier been married to their neighbour, John Tyrell of Herongate. [22]

Anne did not long survive into the new reign. She died in the spring following the coronation, leaving in her will several items of jewellery given her by Mary. She was not buried with John at North Ockendon but in the church of St. Dunstan in the West, Fleet Street, in the city of London, of which her brother-in-law, Thomas Sponer, had been churchwarden. Records of the old church, demolished in the 1830s, describe a gravestone bearing the arms of Poyntz and Sibley. This may well be the stone for which her brother-in-law is recorded as paying. [23]

2. THOMAS POYNTZ AND WILLIAM TYNDALE

i. Thomas Poyntz, Merchant of London and Antwerp

.. where as he bargayned and bought of Thomas Poyntz citizyn and grocer of London 18c of almonds ..

John Crosse Citizen & Woolman of London c1520

The earliest known record of Thomas Poyntz is in 1517 when he rented a house off London's Cheapside from the Hospital of St. Thomas of Acre. At about the same time he was admitted to the freedom of the Grocers' Company.

In 1517 Cheapside was the very heart of the city of London, a noisy and colourful neighbourhood. On great occasions of state crowds would line the sides of the wide street and gather at the windows of the tall houses to watch the passing procession making its way from the Tower to Westminster. Many years earlier Chaucer had written of the apprentice who regularly left his work whenever there was a festival or procession in Cheap. The street echoed to the cries of the sellers in the markets which, as the name implies, had long been a feature of the neighbourhood. Gossip was exchanged whilst collecting water at one or other of the two conduits which would flow with wine on special days. Then there were the pillory and the Standard outside St. Mary-le-Bow, where various grim punishments were often publicly enacted. Another monument was the Cheapside Cross standing at the entrance to Wood Street, the street in which had been the house of Edmund Shaa. Church bells tolled as the dead were carried through the chaotic life of the street to burial in one of the numerous parish churches of the area, whilst at other times the bells would be heard marking the masses and other ceremonies of a medieval church as yet untouched by new ideas from abroad. The view towards the west end of Cheapside was dominated by St. Paul's Cathedral, dating from the 12th and 13th centuries, with its central tower still surmounted by the spire which was to be destroyed by lightening in 1561.

If Thomas Poyntz were able to visit Cheapside today he would find it unrecognisable but for the layout of the area. Despite the Great Fire, the Blitz, and the re-developments of Victorian, post-war and more recent times, the road itself, and many of the streets running from it, still follow the line and width of past centuries.

So, he might be able to discover Ironmonger Lane, a narrow street which leads north from Cheapside towards the Guildhall. This was the street in which he lived for about a decade. The house he rented stood on the east side of the street towards the Cheapside end. To its north was the Church of St. Martin Pomeroy, the site of which is marked today by a courtyard garden. To its south, standing on the corner of Cheapside and Ironmonger Lane, was the hospital of St. Thomas of Acre from whom he rented his house. It would not surprise Thomas to see the Mercers' Hall there today. The Mercers had a long relationship with the hospital. In his time they already occupied some of the property and he may well have been disturbed by the noise of building work they carried out in those years. After the dissolution of the hospital the Mercers acquired the whole site. At the junction with Cheapside was the larger of the two conduits. [24]

For anybody with the Christian name of Thomas the hospital had great significance. In a house on this site was born in 1120 that most famous English saint of the medieval period, Thomas Becket, and here was founded the hospital, a college of brothers, in memory of his supposed miraculous intervention on behalf of the crusaders at the siege of Acre. Today the site is marked by a head and shoulders image of Becket, with an accompanying explanatory plaque, high up on the wall at the corner of Cheapside and Ironmonger Lane.

The hospital had another significance for Thomas. As was mentioned earlier, in its church were buried several of his relations. Most notable his great uncle, Sir Edmund Shaa (1488), and his uncle, Sir John Shaa (1504). This is a reminder that, whilst Thomas Poyntz came from a relatively obscure, albeit locally significant, Essex family, noting the Shaa connection shows how such a family could easily have grander links through marriage. In an England of only about three million people, and in a society where early mortality often led to re-marriages, a network of relationships could soon build up. Social bridges also came about through contact with neighbouring families of similar socio-economic status. So, when Thomas arrived in London he would certainly have had contacts to draw upon and to help establish himself.

Thomas must have seen his future in trade as a merchant so rather than following his father in the Goldsmiths' Company, to which he could presumably have been admitted by patrimony, he turned instead to the the Grocers' Company. This company traces its origins back to 1345 when it was concerned primarily with trade in spices. By Thomas' time its members were engaged in wide ranging wholesale trade. Since 1515 it has been second in order of precedence amongst the city livery companies, one of the so called Great Twelve. Today the company has wide charitable interests, above all in the field of education. The company has had a series of halls on the same site in Princes Street, by the Bank of England, since 1426.

Thomas' age when he arrived in London is unknown but his apprenticeship would likely have been between seven and ten years and, in 1496, the Grocers had made a rule that no apprentice could be admitted to the freedom of the company until they were at least twenty five years of age. Thus it seems likely that Thomas was born in the early 1490s and that he would have been no more than about ten years of age when his mother died.

Thomas' admission to the Grocers is something of a mystery. The records of the company give no details of his admission, his name simply appearing from 1518 in the list of those who paid their annual 'brotherhood money'. The answer may possibly lie in a gap in the list of apprentices admitted in 1517. It appears as if the person writing up the list for the year was unsure of a name, left a blank space intending to insert it later but never did so. The name of the master is given, George Kirkby, the date of admission and the fee but not the name of the apprentice. Perhaps this was Thomas Poyntz. [25]

Thomas continued to pay his annual dues for some eight years but there is little other evidence of his activities. This was a very litigious age and there are two documents surviving from actions in which he was involved. One concerned a supply of almonds which had been ordered from him. [26]

At some point he made a decision to move to Antwerp. The exact date of his departure from London is unknown, although putting together the evidence it was probably in 1526. This date is arrived at by noting a travel document issued to him in December 1525, and the fact that he shortly afterwards ceased to pay his rent and his Grocers' dues. [27]

There is no evidence of how much interest Thomas took in the emerging religious debate of the period. We can only speculate as to whether he walked the few yards from his home to St. Paul's Churchyard on a May day in 1521 and joined the great crowd which saw Thomas Wolsey preside over a burning of the writings of Martin Luther. If he did he can hardly have imagined that there would come a time when he would only just escape with his life after being accused of believing in Luther's teachings. Neither do we know what view he held, if any, on the translation of the Bible into the vernacular. However, about the time he left England a church only minutes walk from his house, All Hallows, Honey Lane, was being turned into a warehouse for banned religious books imported from the continent. These included the first edition of William Tyndale's translation of the New Testament, the first such translation to be printed for mass distribution in England. If Thomas knew of this book he certainly did not know what trouble its translator was to cause him. Many copies of this New Testament, like some other of these books, were arriving from Antwerp, the very place to which he was now moving his interests.

After some ten years living and working in London Thomas Poyntz was to spend the next decade in another great city of commerce. Antwerp was a prosperous city, one of the major centres of trade in Europe. Here many English merchants were based and Poyntz would already know a number of

The corner of Cheapside and Honey Lane. No trace remains of All Hallows Church.

these. Also, he was now in one of the significant centres of the printing industry and book trade. Progress in printing techniques meant that the new ideas which were causing religious controversy across Europe could be spread more rapidly than would have been possible in any past time. In many shipments of goods to England from Antwerp there were smuggled Bibles and other religious literature.

There is no evidence that Thomas Poyntz had any involvement in the smuggling of books and so far as is known he simply went about his business as he had done in London. However, it does appear that at some point he took on an additional responsibility. He is found having a role in the housing arrangements made for English merchants. This may have been connected with his marriage at an unknown date to a local woman, Anna van Calva.

The English merchants in Antwerp were well organised and based in the English House where many of them lived. It has often been assumed that this was where Thomas Poyntz lived and that this was where he was later to entertain William Tyndale. In fact a careful reading of relevant references may suggest otherwise.

The primary source of information about the later entertainment of Tyndale by Poyntz, and the subsequent events, is that given by John Foxe in his *Acts and Monuments*. This massive study of Christian martyrs, including Protestant martyrs of his own time, appeared in various editions from 1563. Where Foxe relates the Tyndale story there is a side heading in the 1570 edition which reads : 'The order and maner of takyng of Tyndall, testified by Poyntz his host'. Certainly the detail of much of this section suggests that it was based upon eye witness accounts.

Foxe wrote that Poyntz : 'kept there (*in Antwerp*) an house of Englyshs marchauntes'. This has often been read as suggesting that Poyntz had some responsibility for the management of the English House, but he was certainly not the governor, and if this was a reference to the English House it might be supposed that Foxe would have said 'the house of English merchants' rather than 'an house'. However, further reading of Foxe's account seems to indicate that this house was one which was much more personally connected with Poyntz. He wrote that Tyndale stayed 'in the house of Thomas Pointz' ; he wrote of 'Pointz sytting at his dore'; and he explained that 'at the going forth of Poyntz house, was a long narrowe entry' . In each of these, and other, references it seems clear that what was being written about was not some apartment within the English House but a completely separate house with its own entrance which was identified as being Poyntz's house, presumably by he himself in talking to Foxe or his representative.

Later when Poyntz wrote to his brother about these events he used similar language to describe the house. He wrote of William Tyndale that he : ' was lodged with <u>me</u>', 'was taken out of <u>my</u> house', and 'has lain in <u>my</u> house'. If this were the English House it seems unlikely that he would so describe it. [28]

In a study published in 1950-4 Oskar De Smet looked at the English in Antwerp at this period. He believed that there were several houses in which English merchants could live. Apart from the main English House there were other approved houses, particularly used by younger merchants. The house of Thomas Poyntz was one of these. This would certainly make sense of the quotations above. [29]

It might seem relatively unimportant and little more than a matter of curiosity whether Poyntz was based in the English House or elsewhere. In fact, this may have relevance to the part he was to play in later events.

As to the meeting of Thomas and Anna, this could have arisen from her being already in the employ of the English merchants in one or other of their houses. Perhaps on arrival in Antwerp it was at a house managed by Anna that Thomas stayed and thus their coming together. Many years later, long after Thomas had left Antwerp, there is evidence of Anna still running this establishment. [30]

By the early fifteen thirties the Poyntz family was growing. The lack of birth and baptismal records make it impossible to be certain about the birth dates of their children but the available evidence suggests that it was probably in 1532 that the eldest child was born. In the light of subsequent events, which removed Thomas from the family home in late 1535, the other three must have followed in fairly quick succession. There were three boys – Gabriel, Ferdinando, and Robert – and one girl – Susannah. [31]

It must have been a busy household with Anna's pregnancies, the care of the children, the entertainment of the merchants who stayed there, and Thomas's own business activities. Then, in addition, in the summer of 1534, Thomas and Anna received another guest, this time not a merchant but the theologian and Bible translator William Tyndale. [32]

ii. The Vision of William Tyndale

I do marvel greatly, dearly beloved in Christ, that ever any man should repugn or speak against the scripture to be had in every language, and that of every man.

William Tyndale The Pathway to Holy Scripture

Whether the paths of Thomas Poyntz and William Tyndale had crossed before the summer of 1534 is quite unknown. Tyndale had spent a year in London around 1523 during the time that Poyntz himself was there and so it is not impossible that they may have met. Later there were periods when Tyndale was in Antwerp and they could have encountered each other in gatherings of the English merchants. However it has to be said that there is absolutely no evidence of any acquaintance between them prior to 1534.

What Poyntz almost certainly did not know, and would probably not have found of any interest at the time, was that when he walked a few yards from his home in Ironmonger Lane into the Church of St. Thomas of Acre, where his Shaa relations lay, he was in the very church where, on Easter Eve 1515, a young man giving his name as William Hychyns was ordained priest. He is described in the register of Bishop FitzJames as being a Bachelor of Arts from the diocese of Hereford. The previous year this man had been ordained a sub-deacon in the diocese of Hereford. That he was William Tyndale is almost certain. Tyndale sometimes described himself as William Hychyns and it seems clear that this was the name he used both as a student at Oxford and as a candidate for ordination. [33]

The reason for the use of the name Hychyns, or Tyndale alias Hychyns, is unknown. This just adds to the obscurity surrounding his family background and early life. The chronicler Edward Hall said that he came from 'about the borders of Wales' which is far from being a precise location. The many who have researched William's family over the years have favoured the idea that he came from Gloucestershire. The village of Stinchcombe was home to various people using the Hychyns and Tyndale names which makes it seems likely that his roots were there but there is a lack of clear information. The position is further confused by the references in the ordination registers which seem to link him with the Hereford diocese in which Gloucestershire west of the Severn then lay. It may be the case that he came of a family that had members on both sides of the river. [34]

In 1515 Tyndale was both ordained priest and awarded his M.A. from Oxford University. The next few years are again something of a mystery. The fact of his being ordained in London might suggest that he had been offered a post there, or at least was seeking one. If so there does not seem to be any record surviving of such an appointment. Possibly he was the William Tyndale who is recorded in these years as a chantry priest in Gloucestershire, first at Frampton on Severn and then at Breadstone. According to the register of the bshop of Worcester this man was dead by 1523 but this could be a clerical error or, indeed, there could have been two men of the same name. John Foxe placed him at Cambridge for several years. Again this is possible but seemingly unrecorded in the university archives. [35]

The Cambridge claim is given by John Foxe (1517-1587) in his book *Acts and Monuments*, commonly called the *Book of Martyrs*. This book provides a detailed account of Tyndale at two periods of his life, in Gloucestershire and London in the early fifteen twenties, and then in Antwerp and Brussels during his last two years, 1534-1536. Foxe had been educated at Oxford but eventually had to resign a fellowship at Magdalen as he was intent on marriage. At Oxford he had become converted to an evangelical position in religion. He was ordained priest late in life, having spent many years writing, translating and compiling a range of religious books. During Mary's reign he was one of those who fled abroad to avoid persecution and it was during that period he compiled the first of a series of books based around the lives of Christian martyrs. This work eventually led him to produce four editions of his *Acts and Monuments*.

Foxe's work is an invaluable source for information about those who fell into difficulties with the authorities as a result of their reformed views in the Tudor period. Of course he was writing from one religious position and that has to be borne in mind in an attempt to differentiate fact from hagiography, and in seeking not to forget those of other persuasions who suffered also. As the various editions of *Acts and Monuments* were issuing from the press many Catholics were being executed as traitors to Elizabeth I, as indeed those of conservative views had been in the time of Henry VIII. Valuable source though it is there is no doubt that the work of Foxe encouraged religious animosities in England.

Foxe obtained his material from a range of sources, some already published but much either extracted from manuscripts, many now lost, or obtained in conversation with those who had known the martyrs. In the case of William Tyndale the presence of detailed information in places does suggest that Foxe was working with associates of the man himself. For the early section the source is unknown. It has been speculated that this was a Richard Webb who certainly provided Foxe with other material and who had been at one time a servant of a future martyr Hugh Latimer, then rector of West Kington, in Somerset but only just over the border from Gloucestershire. For the later years, as mentioned earlier, Foxe states that Thomas Poyntz was one source.

Webb, or somebody else with inside information, must have been the means by which Foxe obtained a fairly detailed account of the years of Tyndale's life from 1522 to 1524. Foxe tells that he was employed by a Gloucestershire man, Sir John Walsh, at his home of Little Sodbury Manor. Walsh was a notable local figure, married at one time to the daughter of Sir Robert Poyntz, and with several young children, the eldest probably no more than four years of age, to whom it is said Tyndale acted as tutor. The role was probably no onerous task and was a way in which the young man could carry on his studies. In this period many scholars who did not hold university appointments looked to well off patrons to give them material support, as in the case of the aid given to Desiderius Erasmus by Lord Mountjoy. John Walsh was just the first of several patrons Tyndale was to attract over the following years. It may be that he was known to, or introduced to, Sir John through his Gloucestershire background and contacts, possibly through a brother Edward who was a significant figure in the area.

When Tyndale was ordained in 1515 it is most unlikely that he foresaw the dramas that were to shake the very foundations of the church in the coming decades. The name of the German Augustinian friar Martin Luther had yet to become a term of abuse, applied indiscriminately to those the church came to consider as heretics and to be thrown at both Tyndale and Poyntz in later years. However, by Tyndale was settled into his life at Little Sodbury the new 'heretical' ideas about theology and worship were circulating in Europe and in England. In 1521 Cardinal Wolsey attended at St. Paul's Cross, by the cathedral in the heart of London, and with great ceremony presided over a burning of Luther's writings. In the same year the king wrote against Luther for which he was to receive from Pope Leo X the title Defender of the Faith.

It is unclear at what point William Tyndale began to find his own thinking moving away in certain respects from the tradition of the church, nor do we know when he conceived the great vision of an English Bible. Certainly whilst he was at Little Sodbury, if not before, Tyndale was of the belief that the scriptures must be made available to the English people in their own language. At this point the Bible was read in church in Latin, the scholarly and ecclesiastical language of Europe, so meaning nothing to the average worshipper. Tyndale's single minded pursuit of his objective determined so much of the remainder of his life. When he found himself in conflict with churchmen in Gloucestershire he decided upon a move to London in the hope that the bishop, Cuthbert Tunstall, would give him a position in his household to replace the patronage of John Walsh and so allow him to begin the translation of which he dreamed.

In this hope he was to be disappointed. However, shortly after arriving in London in 1523 he was approached by a London merchant who had heard him preach. Humphrey Monmouth gave Tyndale board and lodging in his house where the young scholar continued his studies 'lyke a good priest, studying bothe nyght and day'. Later Monmouth was to fall under suspicion as a result of his taking William Tyndale into his house for those six months.

Now in London Tyndale was in a good position to assess whether he might hope for any support in his work towards a Bible in English. As the months passed it became increasingly clear to him that the official attitude in England was, at the best, indifferent to such a project. The association of a Bible in the vulgar tongue with John Wyclif back in the fourteenth century and his followers, the Lollards, who were regarded as heretics, made for a more negative attitude towards translation in England than was commonly the case in mainland Europe. In 1524 Tyndale decided that pursuit of his goal might be best undertaken abroad and so he left London with a little financial backing from Monmouth and other sympathetic merchants.

Over the next ten years Tyndale moved from place to place according to where the needs of his work or security demanded. He may have spent a period at Wittenburg with Martin Luther. By 1525 he had completed his translation of the New Testament and was in Cologne supervising its printing. In an essentially Catholic city this was a dangerous enterprise. It is reckoned that careless talk in the print shop gave the game away. Tyndale took what was already printed and fled to Worms.

It was in Worms in 1526 that the complete text of the New Testament was printed, the first New Testament in English to be mass produced using the printing press rather than being laboriously hand written. As Thomas Poyntz left England to settle in Antwerp the first copies were being smuggled in the opposite direction. [36]

The leading Tyndalian scholar Professor David Daniell has written : 'What had been hidden in Latin for many centuries was now suddenly and for the first time available to everybody'. He has repeatedly drawn attention to the features of Tyndale's work that make it so much more than just a translation of the New Testament into English. In order to do this work Tyndale learnt Greek so that he could translate from the original language. He also used the Latin Vulgate of St. Jerome and the German translation by Martin Luther but essentially his work is based on the original text in so far as Erasmus had been able to compile this. Further significance of this translation lies in it showing the possibility of using the English language for a book of significance, rather than Latin or French as had been the custom. Tyndale's direct English makes his translation very readable even today and he introduced many words and phrases into the developing English language. [37]

By now Tyndale was also writing a series of works both outlining his criticisms of the church as he found it and expounding his theological position. Though influenced in some respects by the teachings of Martin Luther he was no slavish Lutheran, even though that term has often been applied to him from the sixteenth century to the present day. In addition he had somehow managed to learn Hebrew and was working on translating the Old Testament with the aim of publishing a complete Bible in the English tongue. [38]

In these years it is not always clear where he was living and working. He certainly spent some time in Antwerp but at other periods his whereabouts are unknown. Once his New Testaments began to enter England William Tyndale was no longer an obscure scholar. He was now of concern to the authorities. His translation was burnt at St. Paul's Cross, as Luther's writings had been five years earlier. Attempts were made to persuade him to return to England, whether so that the king might use his talents or simply burn him is not always clear. Tyndale suspected the latter and so was wary of doing the king's command. He always maintained that he was loyal to the king but suspected that if he returned the bishops would persuade Henry to treat him badly. He also wanted from Henry an assurance that the king would allow the Bible in English.

Tyndale well knew the dangers of returning. He was engaged in a fierce written dialogue with Sir Thomas More, Lord Chancellor and pursuer of heretics, who made his views of Tyndale's theology very clear. In England men who were sympathetic to Tyndale's ideas, who were involved in book smuggling and distribution, and some of whom had been with him on the Continent, were being burnt at Smithfield. Even his old patron Humphrey Monmouth was taken in for questioning about his support of Tyndale. To be associated with Tyndale or his writings was now dangerous. No wonder that the man himself thought it wisest to remain 'in the parts beyond the seas'.

From late 1529 Tyndale was back in Antwerp. From here the following year the first part of his Old Testament translation from the Hebrew began to be taken into England, the five books of the Pentateuch, the only part of the Old Testament to be published in his lifetime. [39]

With both his translations and other writings William Tyndale was now the most significant Englishman in the movement we know as the Reformation. This was the man who took up lodgings with Thomas and Anna Poyntz in the summer of 1534.

William Tyndale, Millennium Square, Bristol by Lawrence Holofcener 2000.

3. AT THE HOUSE OF THOMAS POYNTZ

i. Tyndale at Work

He was a man very frugal and spare of body, a great student, an earnest labourer in the setting forth of the scripture.

John Foxe

William Tyndale had long been asked for a second, corrected and improved, edition of his New Testament. In the summer of 1534 his former assistant George Joye edited a new edition as Tyndale himself seemed to have taken little action in the matter. This infuriated Tyndale. Joye had not consulted him and had not made clear his own responsibility for changes to the text. These changes Tyndale believed to be quite inaccurate. He set to work to produce his own revision. He needed somewhere safe and quiet to get on with this task as a matter of urgency and this place was to be in the household of Thomas Poyntz.[40]

It should have been a relatively safe place for him. Whatever the heresy laws in force in Antwerp it was in general a much more relaxed city in this regard than in many other parts of the Holy Roman Empire. The authorities were particularly likely to be lenient with English merchants in view of their economic value to the city. So long as Tyndale remained in a house linked with the English merchant community he was unlikely to be troubled.

There is no record of where he had been living previously. Possibly he had been at the main English House. It seems likely that the governor of The English House at this moment was Humphrey Monmouth who had given support to Tyndale back in London in 1523 and 1524. If this is correct it is possible that Tyndale had been a guest in the English House and that when Monmouth's term of duty expired in July 1534, and he was no longer in such regular contact with Antwerp, he looked for someone to take over the role of Tyndale's host. The new governor, or other merchants, may have been less happy at having such a known heretic in their midst. [41]

For Poyntz to have taken Tyndale into his home suggests that he had some sympathy with the work in which his new guest was engaged. As noted earlier, there appears to be no evidence that Tyndale and Poyntz had any acquaintance prior to this time. Tyndale had been in London for some months before leaving England, when Poyntz was still at Ironmonger Lane, and he had been in Antwerp for significant periods of time prior to 1534. However, nowhere in Poyntz's accounts, as given either to Foxe or to his brother, is there any indication of previous contact with Tyndale.

Tyndale was described as being at this time 'a man very frugal and spare of body, an earnest laborer, namely in the setting forth of the scriptures of God'. Once settled in the Poyntz household he would have been concentrating on the revised New Testament which was finally published in November 1534. This translation has been described by David Daniell as 'the glory of his life's work'. Once this was completed Tyndale would have turned back to continue his translation from Hebrew of the Old Testament books. Much had already been done but much remained to do. Of this moment David Daniell has written : 'The rest of the Bible lay ahead of him. Tyndale might well have had high hopes'.[42]

During these months there were no doubt many visitors who came to talk with Tyndale. Foxe tells of the visits of Henry Phillips, of whom more later. His dark shadow was to fall increasingly over the Poyntz home.

Another visitor was George Constantine. Involved in the distribution of the 1526 New Testament in England, Constantine had first fled to Antwerp in 1528 after being named as an associate of Thomas Bilney, then under interrogation and imprisonment by Wolsey for supposedly holding Lutheran views. He had returned to England in 1530, only to be taken in for questioning by the Lord Chancellor and great pursuer of heresy, Thomas More, to whom he had given names and details connected with the importation of forbidden books. Allowed to escape, he had hastened back to Antwerp. It seems that, once More fell from favour, and was in the Tower of London, Constantine felt it safe to return to England. He must have become quite close to the Poyntz family, possibly through visits to Tyndale, for he took with him back to England Ferdinando, the second son of Thomas and Anna, 'for his education in learning and good manners'. Constantine was back in England by May 1535 when he witnessed the executions of Ann Boleyn and those who died with her. [43]

In 1537 there appeared the so called 'Matthew's Bible', the first which Henry VIII allowed to be licensed and dedicated to him. Based wherever possible on Tyndale's translations, this is considered to be the work of John Rogers. Whilst there is no specific evidence linking him with Poyntz or his house, it seems almost certain that he would have been another visitor in those months.

Rogers had been incumbent of the church of Holy Trinity the Less, Knightrider Lane, in London and had moved to Antwerp as chaplain to the English merchant community in 1534. Here, according to Foxe : 'It chaunced him ther to fal in company with that worthy martir of God Wylliam Tindal, & with Miles Couerdale … In conferryng with them the scriptures, he came to great knowledge in the Gospel of God, in so much that he cast of the heauy yoke of popery, perceiuing it to be impure & filthy idolatry & ioyned him self with them two in that painful & most profitable labor of traslating þe bible into the English tongue'. [44]

David Daniell considers it likely that Rogers knew Greek and Hebrew and that he may have worked with Tyndale in late 1534 and early 1535.

Rogers's nineteenth century biographer tried to imagined the scene : 'It is no idle fancy to imagine these two friends, seated in Tyndale's private study in the hospitable house of Thomas Poyntz, discussing points of doctrine tending to the conversion and confirmation of the new comer in the Protestant faith, and subsequently to behold them both busily engaged in rendering into their own language the pages of that Sacred Volume which, till then, had been a sealed book to their countrymen'. [45]

Rogers was destined to become the first to die in the burnings of Queen Mary's reign.

Foxe mentioned Miles Coverdale as also working with Tyndale at this time and he could well have been another visitor to the Poyntz's house. In 1535 he was to produce an English Bible in Antwerp whilst Tyndale languished in prison.

The Poyntz household must have been a place of many comings and goings of those who were involved with Tyndale's work or wished to talk with him. The security this house offered probably made it safer to meet there than in some other parts of the city, although that is not to say that Tyndale did not go out and about. Indeed, had he not been willing to do so he would not have been arrested.

According to John Foxe he was in the habit of giving over two days a week to visiting and assisting both religious refugees from England and the local poor. The other activity, described in the same source, seems very probable. 'When the Sunday came, then went he to some one merchants' chamber or other, whither came many other merchants, and unto them would he read some one parcel of scripture : the which proceeded so fruitfully, sweetly, and gently from him .. that it was a heavenly comfort and joy to the audience to hear him read the scriptures; likewise, after dinner, he spent an hour in the same manner.'

The future for which William Tyndale no doubt hoped at this time was a lifetime of study, translating, revising, writing, and preaching and this expectation might have been but for the arrival of the mysterious figure of Henry Phillips.

ii. Betrayed by Henry Phillips

About which time came thither one out of England, whose name was Henry Phillips .... but wherefore he came, or for what purpose he was sent thither, no man could tell.

John Foxe

Foxe's account of the events associated with Henry Phillips makes clear that his sudden appearance was unexplained and, to a large extent, remained so when Foxe was collecting material for his book some twenty and more years later. This suggests that his source, Thomas Poyntz, was never able to made full sense of Phillips, although he probably had more opportunity than anybody to observe the man and his actions. That Phillips engineered the arrest of Tyndale, and then of Poyntz, is clear. On the other hand so many questions about his activities remain unanswered.

The main sources from which to try and disentangle Phillips's life are the account of Foxe and correspondence both from and about Phillips. The letters from him must presumably have been intercepted by the English authorities as they are to family and friends, not correspondence that would normally be found amongst state papers in the National Archives.

Henry Phillips' family home was in Dorset, at Charborough near Poole. His father, Richard, was a significant local figure, at various times a member of Parliament and sheriff of Dorset. He held a position in relation to leasing of tolls around Poole Harbour. This background gave Henry a sophisticated appearance. Foxe wrote that he was : 'a comely fellowe lyke as he hadde bene a gentleman hauing a seruaunt with hym'.

The evidence suggests that Henry was well educated. According to Foxe he was described by Tyndale as 'hamsomly learned'. He is believed to have attended Oxford and graduated BCL in 1533 and in three of his surviving letters he wrote extensively in Latin. Amongst those from whom he sought help when in difficulty were Dr. Thomas Brerewood, archdeacon of Barnstaple and chancellor to the Bishop of Exeter – described by Thomas, Lord Audley, as a scholar - and a Dr. Underhill, who may have been one of that name holding prebends in the diocese of Salisbury and in the royal chapel of St. Stephen at Westminster. Phillips gave no hint as to how he knew these two men but he seemed to assume that his mother would know who they were. Perhaps they were family contacts or figures encountered in his education. In one letter he commented on the respect which his parents had for Brerewood and he wrote of this man as if he had been some sort of tutor or mentor. [46]

According to a much later letter to his mother, some months after he left Oxford he was sent by his father on a business errand to London carrying a sum of money. In the course of his journey he lost his father's money at gaming, and also lost his own money intended for his expenses. He was afraid to return and face his father. He refers to having visited a Mr. Semer. Presumably this was to discuss his situation but he gave no details of any conversation with this man. It has been suggested that this was the same Mr. Semer who at the time was incumbent of his home parish in Dorset. [47]

The next mention of Phillips is not until December 1534 when he is recorded as having matriculated at the University of Leuven. Sadly, there seems no information as to what happened in the intervening months and how he came to be at this university, well known for attracting Englishmen of a religiously conservative disposition. [48]

By now Tyndale was living with the Poyntz family and, if Foxe is correct, he brought Phillips to the house after having met him at the homes of various other merchants to which he had been invited to dine. As well as sharing some meals with the Poyntz family it appears that on occasion he may have stayed overnight. He obviously impressed Tyndale but not Poyntz. According to Foxe : 'Poyntz hauinge no great confidence in the fellowe, asked maister Tyndall who brought hym or howe he came acquainted with Henry Philippes'. Tyndale assured him that Phillips was 'an honest man, hansomly learned, & very confirmable'.

On one occasion Phillips asked Poyntz to walk with him and to show him the sights of the town. As they talked it became clear that Phillips had some plan afoot. Later Poyntz realised that Phillips had been hoping for his help in return for money. He boasted of having money, the source of which Foxe described as unknown.

In Foxe's account events then moved rapidly. Instead of enlisting the help of the authorities in Antwerp and risking his plan becoming known, Phillips went to Brussels and persuaded the procurer general to return with him to Antwerp. Foxe commented : 'The whiche was not done with small charges and expences, from whom so euer it came'.

No doubt Phillips had planned carefully the timing of his move. He must have known that the merchants would be out of town for several weeks at a fair in a Bergen op Zoom some distance away. The first time he checked Poyntz was still at home. He waited and then returned a few days later.

He asked Anna what she was serving for dinner. Then he went away. Returning later he first borrowed some money from Tyndale, claiming to have lost his purse on the way. Then he said that he would stay and dine but Tyndale should be his guest. Tyndale explained that he was dining out but that Phillips would be welcome to accompany him. Perhaps Phillip's complicated manoeuvres, including the lunch invitation Tyndale had received, were all part of a plan – first to avoid suspicion and then to trap Tyndale.

Outside the door was a narrow passage at the end of which Phillips had two men waiting, maybe bribed with the money he had earlier borrowed from Tyndale. Phillips was the taller of the two men and, standing behind his victim, pointed that this was the man to be taken. In seconds Tyndale was in their hands and on his way to Vilvoorde Castle. Later the procurer general went to the house and removed Tyndale's books and other possessions. The suspicions Thomas Poyntz had entertained about Phillips were now fully realised.

The comments of Foxe about the money Phillips had to pursue this matter emphasise one of its mysterious elements. At the time Poyntz wrote of the 'papists' and Hall, in his Chronicles, wrote of 'some bishops of this realm' but these are very general descriptions. Whilst names have been suggested as to who initiated and financed the plot, there is no evidence clearly pointing to any identifiable person or group of people. Neither is it at all apparent as to how Phillips became involved. Perhaps in London he encountered somebody who thought that this impecunious but also presentable and educated man would be just the person to infiltrate both the merchant community and Tyndale's circle, or maybe he was recruited after arriving at Leuven. Whatever the truth, he had carried out the first part of the plan. Now he had to pursue it to the desired conclusion, the elimination of William Tyndale. [49]

In tracking the attempts made to help Tyndale over the following months much has to be worked out from clues in surviving correspondence. Unfortunately the really significant diplomatic letters are lost and their existence is only known of through references in other correspondence and in Foxe. However, there does survive one very full letter written by Thomas Poyntz in the matter of Tyndale.

iii. An Appeal to England

a poor man that has no promotion nor looks for none, having no quality whereby he might obtain honour but of a very natural zeal and fear of God and his prince, had liefer live a beggar all days of his life and put himself in jeopordy to die rather than to live and see those leering curs to have their purpose.

Thomas Poyntz to his brother 1535

There is no record as to whether Anna Poyntz sent an immediate message to her husband telling him of the arrest or whether she awaited his return. Foxe wrote of the merchants as sending urgent letters to Brussels in defence of Tyndale. His account then gives the impression that diplomatic correspondence began to fly between Brussels and London. In fact, on the basis of available evidence, little activity of this type seems to have taken place until the early autumn. Perhaps it was expected that the matter could be resolved locally. Poyntz later criticised the governor of the English House for not having pursued it vigorously enough.

By the second half of August it seems that Thomas was despairing of the situation. On the 21st he wrote a letter to England. It was addressed to his brother John at the family home at North Ockendon in Essex.. This document survives in the British Library. [50]

Unfortunately the letter has suffered some damage and is an unhelpfully bound volume of papers. The right hand side of two pages has been scorched at some time, whilst the other page is too closely bound for the last word(s) of each sentence to be seen.

The letter runs to around thirteen hundred words. It argues a clear case, basically that William Tyndale was a loyal subject of Henry VIII but that the conservatives in the English church had schemed to destroy him by 'crafty juggling' including deceiving the king. His death would be detrimental to the cause of the gospel.

In the preceding months Thomas must have heard, and joined with, Tyndale in discussion. When he sat down to write he may have planned it with assistance from one or more of those others who had been visiting the house and participating in those conversations. If this was the case then John Rogers seems a likely candidate. Thus, it is not surprising that some of the argument in the letter, and aspects of its presentation, echo William Tyndale. In particular there are several reminders of Tyndale's book of 1528 *The Obedience of a Christian Man.* [51]

Extract from the letter of Thomas Poyntz to John Poyntz August 1535. In modern spelling this reads :

// for whereas it was said here the king had granted his gracious letters in the favour of one William Tyndall for to have been sent hither the which is in prison and like to suffer death except it be through his gracious help it is thought those letters be stopped // this man was lodged with me three quarters of a year and was taken out of my house by a sergeant of arms otherwise a door warder and the procurator general of Brabant the which was done (by) procurement out of England // and as I suppose unknown to the king's grace till done // for I know well if it had pleased his grace to have sent him a command to come into England he would not have disobneyed to have put his life (in) jeopardy //

Reproduced by permission of both the British Library (Cotton Galba Bx.60) and the City of London Guildhall Library (facsimile in its copy of J.A.Kingdon *Incidents in the life of Thomas Poyntz and Richard Grafton…* 1895).

A major theme of *The Obedience* is the concept of duty. Each person has a responsibility to obey God and also, within this world, those placed over them. Tyndale wrote of the obedience required within the family, of children to their parents, of wives to their husbands. In wider society he made a special point of emphasising the duty of obedience required to the sovereign, which he placed above any obedience demanded by the church authorities. He wrote scathingly of the leaders of the church and claimed that they had used princes to their own ends.

Thomas Poyntz, in his letter, placed great emphasis on the issue of duty and obedience. He began by speaking of his own sense of duty owed to the king and gave this as his reason for writing, rather than immediately raising the issue of Tyndale. He was giving a warning, that those engaged in this plot were in fact seeking their own ends 'under colour of pretending the king's honour and yet be as thorns under a godly rose, I might say very traitors in their hearts'. Whilst he named no particular persons, he suggested that they were 'the papists which have always been the deceivers of the world by their crafty juggling'. The phrase 'crafty juggling' appears in various forms in *The Obedience* and seems to have been a favourite way in which Tyndale spoke of those who wished to retain loyalty to the papacy.

The letter then introduced the situation in which Tyndale was at that moment, 'in prison and like to suffer death'. Poyntz had heard rumours that the king had interceded on Tyndale's behalf but that at some point these letters had been stopped.

He went on to describe to his brother how Tyndale had lodged with him for the previous nine months and had been taken out of his house by the procurer general of Brabant. Whilst again he made no specific accusation, he seemed clear that this action had been planned from England 'and as I suppose unknown to the King's Grace till done'. Throughout the letter Poyntz constantly put Henry in a good light. Whether this was altogether sincere, or whether he was simply being diplomatic, it is impossible to say.

There then follows a section in which Thomas Poyntz introduced for the first time his belief in the loyalty of Tyndale to his king. He was in no doubt that if the king had asked Tyndale to return to England he would have obeyed. However, the conservatives in the church feared that Henry might then listen to Tyndale and so had engineered his arrest and then persuaded the king that this was in his interest. This part of the letter includes some strong criticism of these people, who Poyntz saw as seeking their own personal ends. [52]

The letter then becomes quite personal. Poyntz wrote of himself : 'a poor man that has no promotion nor looks for none, having no quality whereby he might obtain honour but of a very natural zeal and fear of God and his prince, had liefer live a beggar all days of his life and put himself in jeopordy to die rather than to live and see those leering curs to have their purpose, for some men perceive more than they can express by words the which sorrow it inwardly till they see remedy'. [53]

Poyntz then returned to the issue of Tyndale's loyalty to Henry of which he knew from their contact over the previous months. He wrote that Tyndale : 'does know that he is bound by the law of God to obey his prince. I wot it well that he would not do the contrary to be made lord of the world howsoever the king's grace be informed'. By contrast he wrote of the bad record of the 'papists' in achieving their ends by any means, including 'shedding the blood of innocents' and persuading princes to go along with them. All this is very reminiscent of *The Obedience*.

Then the letter praises Henry with a Biblical comparison of a type commonly used by Tyndale. It must be a possibility that this was an example that Tyndale himself had been heard to use.

Poyntz reminded his brother of the high priest, Caiaphas, at a meeting of Jewish leaders after the raising of Lazarus. In the words of Tyndale's 1534 translation : 'Then gathered the high priests and the Pharisees a council, and said : what do we? This man doth many miracles. If we let him scape thus, all men will believe on him, and the Romans shall come and take away our country and the people. And one of them named Caiaphas which was the High Priest that same year, said unto them : Ye perceive nothing at all nor yet consider that *it is expedient for us, that one man die for the people*, and not that all the people perish'. [54]

To Christians the idea of one man, Jesus, dying for the people was important but not with the meaning of Caiaphas. So, Poyntz wrote, the king had been given by the Pope the title Defender of the Faith in the belief that Henry would wage war against the new teachings but the contrary was happening, he was becoming the defender of these ideas. 'Never prince has done so nobly since Christ died.' This was perhaps an over optimistic assessment of Henry's standpoint at that time!

Having, for the first time in the letter, introduced the religious issues quite directly, Poyntz then returned to Tyndale and wrote that his death 'should be a great hindrance to the gospel'. He again suggested that if the king invited Tyndale to England to discuss his ideas he would doubtless obey and there might be a useful outcome. He made no suggestion as to how this might come about whilst Tyndale lay in prison.

Thomas finally turned to his brother, requesting him to bring the matter to the king's attention as best he could. Again he made a reference to his personal knowledge of Tyndale and suggested that the king should regard him as a 'high treasure' and that there 'be not many perfecter men this day living'.

It is a planned letter with an argument designed to appeal to the king. However, Thomas had addressed it to his brother, not to Henry, and not even to the king's right hand man, Thomas Cromwell.

Thomas did not ask John to send the letter on to the king or Cromwell, although he made clear that he wanted the king to know what he had written. John was left to decide how to act. The sending of the letter to John with the request that 'this matter may be solicited to his grace' suggests that Thomas believed his brother to be in a position to promote Tyndale's cause, whether directly or through contacts, in a way he himself could not do from Antwerp.

Any connections of John which might have led him to have influence with the king or Cromwell in 1535 are not immediately apparent. By this time his name seems barely on record but earlier it was noted how easily a family such as his could have useful links through marriages, friendships and neighbours to higher reaches of society. John may have had such connections of which any written details have been lost. One possibility is that of contacts arising from his marriage to Anne and thus a Kent connection to the Cheyney and Wyatt families, although there can be no certainty about this. Also, it may be worth noting that, although usually associated with Kent, Anne Boleyn's family did have Essex links. Anne's brother, George, held the title of Viscount Rochford and, in connection with his official duties, lived at some times at Beaulieu Palace near Chelmsford from which Princess Mary was evicted to make room for him.

Thomas' letter to his brother would take almost a month to reach North Ockendon. In the meanwhile he became involved in more official action.

Probably in the same week that Poyntz wrote his letter the most powerful man in England after the king, Thomas Cromwell, also sat down to write. He was with the court on a long summer progress which had taken it to the west of England. Finding a quiet moment he jotted down a list of things 'to do'. Amongst his notes is a reminder to ask the king whether he should write letters about Tyndale. This certainly suggests that pressure was still being brought on Tyndale's behalf from some quarter. Presumably the king's answer was 'yes' as in the next few days Cromwell did indeed write two letters. [55]

Cromwell wrote to two significant figures in the Low Countries, the Marquis of Bergen and the Archbishop of Palermo. We can only guess at the contents. Unfortunately the letters themselves are lost. However, putting together some surviving correspondence to Cromwell with Foxe's account allows us to gather some idea of what then happened.

The Marquis of Bergen had left on a diplomatic mission to Denmark. The merchants arranged to send his letter after him by the hand of Thomas Poyntz. Presumably this indicates that Poyntz was recognised as having a special involvement with Tyndale, which he certainly did if Tyndale had been arrested from his house. He soon caught up with the Marquis who was at first rather off hand with Poyntz, reminding him of the recent burnings in London of anabaptists from Flanders. The following morning, however, the Marquis was in better mood. After breakfast he chatted with Poyntz and then gave him a letter for the Archbishop of Palermo asking him to deal with the matter in consultation with the Regent and Council . [56]

The reply to this initiative was then brought by Thomas Poyntz from Brussels.

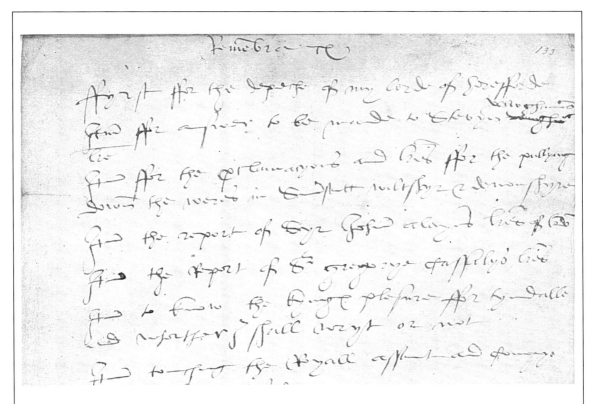

Cromwells' Remembrancer August 1535. Lines 7/8 in modern spelling read :

Item To know the king's pleasure for Tyndalle and whether I shall write or not

Reproduced by permission of The National Archives (E36/143).

to England late in September. Again the contents are unknown to us. Poyntz must have arrived within a few days of his brother receiving the letter written in Antwerp in August. John received that letter on the 20th September and the following day he sent it on to Thomas Cromwell with a covering note.

When he wrote John was not at North Ockendon but at the nearby village of Horndon on the Hill, just possibly trading with Dutch wool merchants who did business there. He was restrained in his wording but emphasised Thomas' belief that the matters of which he had written should come to the attention of the king and council, ' and I according to my bounden duty have sent here the self same letter containing the matter for my discharge and thereupon to determine your pleasure'. [57]

Cromwell now had before him both the reply from the authorities in the Low Countries, and also the letter Thomas Poyntz had written to his brother.

On 28th September the royal summer progress ended with ceremonies at Winchester. The court now returned to London and Cromwell may have then

Letter from John Poyntz to Thomas Cromwell forwarding his brother's letter regarding the plight of William Tyndale, September 1535. In modern spelling this reads :

After due recommendations it may please your mastership to unerstand that the 20th day of this month of September I received this letter here enclosed from a poor man a brother of mine inhabiting in the parts beyond the sea at Antwerp as appeareth by the said letter wherein he writeth to me of things that he would should come to the king's graces knowledge and his council and I according to my bounden duty have sent here the self same letter containing the matter for my discharge and thereupon to determine your pleasure and thus I take my leave of your mastership written at Horndon of the Hill in Essex the 21st day of this present month

Yours with my service
John Poyntz

Reproduced by permission of The National Archives (SP1/196/208).

taken the opportunity to speak personally with Poyntz. Whilst we can only speculate, it could be that any such discussion touched on the possibility of Poyntz playing a more serious role in resolving the issue than simply being a courier. According to Foxe, when he returned to Brussels with Cromwell's reply in late October he was given to understand that Tyndale would be released into his hands.

iv. Poyntz In Fear of His Life

Phillips ... knew none other remedy but to accuse Poyntz, saying that he was a dweller in the town of Antwerp, and there had been a succourer of Tyndale, and was of the same opinion.

John Foxe

Unfortunately Henry Phillips, always listening at an open door, heard of this possibility. Immediately he lodged accusations against Poyntz that he too was a heretic. Some time in November Thomas Poyntz was arrested. The scheme to involve him in a negotiated release of Tyndale nearly proved fatal for him. Phillip's concern to remove Poyntz suggests that he saw this merchant as pivotal to a resolution of the issue. There is no sign of a queue of other merchants lining up to take his place.

If there was a plan for Poyntz to accept responsibility for Tyndale this idea may have been his own or it may have come from the English merchants, Thomas Cromwell, or the authorities in Brussels. Foxe wrote that one reason he expected help from the merchants was that 'thei put hym therto them selfes'. As to Cromwell, presumably he must have agreed to the plan and yet there seems no evidence of any attempt from England to help Poyntz once he was arrested.

Foxe provides a full account of what followed. It seems that he was not held in a prison but guarded by two officers in one of their homes. He was allowed no contact with Antwerp and all conversation and correspondence had to be in Dutch so that it could be understood by the guards. The authorities demanded his answers to a series of questions, initially about 'the kynges affayres as of the message of Tyndal, of his ayders and of Religion'. Using delaying tactics Poyntz managed to avoid giving answers for some weeks but by Christmas he was coming under great pressure and realised that he must answer. Once this process was complete he hoped to be allowed his freedom with surety. However, the financial demands for his release increased, and also he was being ordered to pay for the wages and food of his two guards as well as his own board. According to Foxe he expected help from the English merchants at Antwerp but this was not forthcoming.

By February 1536 'he perceiued his tarying there shoulde haue bene his death' and he decided to make his escape. Foxe recorded that he was pursued but, using his knowledge of the area, he escaped to England. His goaler was fined and the other debts were left unpaid - things that were to come back to haunt Poyntz. [58]

The English authorities seem to have shown no significant further interest in the fate of Tyndale or Poyntz but they had become concerned about Henry Phillips.

According to Foxe, Phillips obtained yet more money and remained around Brussels and 'followed with most diligent attendance' every stage of the proceedings against Tyndale for the eighteen months that remained until the execution.

Here Foxe appears to be wrong. Poyntz, assuming him to be the informant, may have misunderstood what then happened, being himself back in England and not able to observe events at first hand. There is clear evidence that Phillips seems to have suddenly abandoned his project and fled the area.

It must be a possibility that this move was in some way associated with Poyntz's escape. It might be thought that Phillips would be glad to see the back of Poyntz, somebody about whom he would no longer need to bother. Maybe he was afraid that Poyntz could now cause trouble for him, either amongst the merchants in Antwerp, about whose attitude towards him he was said to have been concerned some months earlier, or when he reached England. [59]

Whatever the reason, it appears that, within a few weeks of Poyntz's escape, Phillips was in France trying to ingratiate himself with the daughters of Lady Lisle. He met with Mary and, through her, sent a gift to Philippa on the excuse that they shared similar names. The girls' stepfather was deputy of Calais and the Lisles were known as conservatives in religion. [60]

His stay in France was short, as six weeks later, in early May, he is found in Rome trying to pass himself off as a relation of Sir Thomas More. [61]

The Lisles may have proved unhelpful, or it could be that his rapid journey south was occasioned by news from London. Only a few days after he seems to have been in France in mid-March the English authorities began an attempt to arrest him. Several letters survive, issued in the king's name, and addressed to towns in Germany, with one to the Emperor Charles V, requesting that Phillips be taken. He was then thought to be travelling in Germany with another wanted man. Phillips is described as a 'rebel', and, in the letter to Charles, the two men are said to have 'committed grievous crimes against the king and their neighbours'. [62]

Why the English authorities became so concerned at this point is unclear. It may have had something to do with information Poyntz was able to give on his return, it may have been because Phillips seems to have linked up with a man wanted as a traitor, or for some other reason. The mysteries surrounding Phillips make it uncertain how his actions were viewed by the authorities in England. However, by the next winter he was back in the Brussels area. When he returned, and whether he was there for Tyndale's execution, is unrecorded.

That winter he wrote pleading letters to family and friends in England. He sought forgiveness for the loss of his father's money, denied rumours of disloyalty to his country, and asked for a family member to visit him in Leuven. His main concern seems to have been to obtain financial help for another three years of study. If he had financial backers they had now dropped him despite the success of his mission. [63]

The English authorities continued to pursue him without success. Eventually he was caught up in Henry's final attack on Reginald Pole, later to be Queen Mary's archbishop of Canterbury, his family and acquaintances. The king saw the Pole family as a threat to his throne because of their Plantagenet blood and Reginald's hostility to Henry's marital and religious policies. The most casual or remote contact with Pole was sufficient to bring condemnation as a traitor. In 1539 the *Act of Attainder of the Marquess of Exeter and others* included many great names, and many others quite insignificant. In this last category came Henry Phillips, attainted because he had 'of late wilfully maliciously and traitorously named and pronounced that venemous serpent the Bishop of Rome to be supreme head of the church of ..... England'. Certainly he could not now return to his home country. He is last recorded in Vienna in 1542, suspected of working for the Turks. [64]

4. THE BANISHMENT OF THOMAS POYNTZ

i. 1536

Now Syr, because that she was a favorer of Gods word, at the least wise so taken, I tell you few men wold beleve that she was so abhominable.

George Constantine on the execution of Anne Boleyn

Later, in describing his situation to Henry VIII, Poyntz wrote that he had 'left all his goods beyond the seas' and was 'for matters of religion banished all the emperor's countries upon pain of his head'. It sounds as if he arrived in England with no possessions beyond the clothes he wore and certainly he was without his wife and children. [65]

Having recounted the events of 1535/6 Foxe concluded : 'But what more trouble followeth to Poyntz after the same, it serveth not for this place to rehearse'. This seems to imply that Foxe had material which he did not use and which unfortunately is now seemingly lost.

What trouble did follow to Thomas Poyntz in the eighteen years until he inherited the family estates can be pieced together to some extent from a number of documents which survive, mainly in the National Archives. Valuable though these are in building a picture of those years, they still leave many questions unanswered. However, they do show us a man who suffered much financial and family trouble as a result of his escape from custody, an action he would not have had to take but for his central position in the efforts to save Tyndale and the danger this posed to his life.

There is no record as to whether Thomas Poyntz felt able to make any further representations on Tyndale's behalf after returning to England but there is no significant evidence of any more attempts by the king or Council to intervene. In England men's minds were increasingly occupied by the latest domestic drama. If Thomas had hoped that Anne Boleyn might have pressured Cromwell for action, as she had done in the case of an English merchant of Antwerp some months before, then it was too late. Anne's star was falling as rapidly as the sword of the executioner of Calais was to fall on Tower Green on 19th May. [66]

There is no evidence as to where Poyntz stayed on arrival back in England nor to whom he may have looked for aid.

The execution of Anne Boleyn was witnessed by his friend George Constantine who took a note of what Anne and her associates said on the scaffold. It can only be speculation as to whether Poyntz accompanied him that day. [67]

Copy of Tyndale's translation of the New Testament which belonged to Queen Anne Boleyn. This is the 1534 edition, completed whilst Tyndale was staying with the Poyntz family.

© British Library Board (E50001-69 C.23.a.8, second title page)

In the autumn Thomas must have heard the news of his former lodger having been executed outside Vilvoorde Castle. According to Foxe, on the day of his death, Tyndale gave a letter to the chief keeper of the castle which subsequently he took to Poyntz's house in Antwerp. The fact that Foxe mentions the letter but gives no detail suggests that Poyntz knew of it but had not seen or heard the contents as. In the 1570 edition of *Acts and Monuments* Foxe recorded that the letter was said to be in the possession of the keeper's daughter. Perhaps her father declined to leave the letter as Poyntz was no longer in Antwerp (although surely he knew of the escape before he went to the house) or maybe Anna was wary of accepting a letter from a high profile and condemned heretic. Not knowing Anna's attitude to her husband's involvement with the case of William Tyndale makes it impossible to judge her likely reaction.

Only weeks after the execution of Tyndale, there occurred in London another event of which Poyntz would certainly know and which may again have been linked to the religious situation of the time. Early on the foggy morning of the 13th November Robert Packington, a London merchant and upper warden of the Mercers's Company, was crossing Cheapside on his way to mass in the church of St. Thomas of Acre when, to quote the Mercers' minutes, he 'was piteously slain and murdered with a gun'. His funeral at St. Pancras, Soper Lane, included a sermon from Robert Barnes. Henry Phillips had named Barnes as another man he was after and shortly before the shooting Martin Luther had heard that Barnes was in danger and keeping a low profile. [68]

Who lay behind this shooting and the reason for it is uncertain. It does seem likely that it may have had something to do with Packington's known religious position. As a member of parliament for the city of London he had spoken critically of the clergy and there is a suggestion that he was involved in the import of forbidden religious literature. It may be speculated as to whether his shooting could have been part of a wider plot against heresy, possibly even linked with that which brought about the death of William Tyndale. [69]

Overall this was an uncertain time for those sympathetic to the new religious ideas. Some may well have felt the executioner's sword on Tower Hill and the assassin's bullet in Cheapside to be warnings of the need for care. However, despite the various problems to be faced by Thomas Poyntz arising from his past actions, there is no evidence that, back in England, he suffered any persecution directly as a result of his association with Tyndale. Maybe he trod a careful path, as many others must have done at this time.

ii. A Family Divided

... he trusts his trouble your lordship has in remembrance, the long continuance and the occasion thereof.

Thomas Poyntz to Thomas Cromwell 1539

The surviving documents do not provide details of the day to day life of Poyntz in the following years. It is impossible to tell from these whether he worked at all, where he lived, or what support, if any, he may have had from friends or family.

The first two documents from this period are letters that he himself wrote. Both of these concern his family. They show that he was anxious to bring his wife and children to England and to re-establish their family life together. They suggest concern that he was not able to fulfill his duty as a husband and father.

The first is not dated but internal evidence suggests that it was written in late 1539, three years after his return to England. It was written at a time when the religious houses were being dissolved and petitioners were addressing letters to Thomas Cromwell seeking land and property from the dissolved foundations. [70]

Poyntz wrote of : 'the honour of God and the truth of his word for the which I have suffered this persecution five years'. Maybe he felt that Cromwell owed him something having probably been involved in the decision to release Tyndale to him. After all, it was this plan which had been the trigger for Phillips engineering his arrest.

Thomas then turned to his family, 'my poor wife and infant children'. He would spare Cromwell a lengthy account of his feelings about his family situation but did not doubt that Cromwell would feel compassion for them if he expressed everything he felt.

At the moment he could not provide for them but looked forward to doing so in the future. He was writing to Cromwell to ask if he could 'have the keeping of some suppressed house, as Holywell or some other at your lordships pleasure, that be the mean whereof I might have some honest free dwelling here for me my wife and my children till I may otherwise provide'.

The reference to Holywell helps to date the letter as this may well be a reference to Holywell Priory in Shoreditch which was dissolved in October 1539. Why Poyntz asked about this house in particular is not explained. The prioress had surrendered to William Petre who was in the process of becoming a close neighbour of the Poyntz family in Essex through acquiring land at Ingatestone from Barking Abbey. [71]

There is no evidence that Cromwell took any action on this request. Unlike many others writing in to Cromwell about the estates of religious houses at this time, Thomas Poyntz was in no position to offer any financial inducement.

The next letter is again undated but is probably from 1541. This was written to Henry VIII and concerned two of the sons of Thomas and Anna. Thomas explained to the king how he had sent Ferdinando to England in 1535 in the care of George Constantine with the intention that he should be placed at school in Burton Upon Trent. At this time Ferdinando cannot have been more than eighteen months old. How exactly he was to be cared for is unclear as Constantine himself, although he had Staffordshire links, seems to have been around London and in service with Henry Norris. After Norris's execution in the matter of Ann Boleyn, Constantine moved to Wales. [72]

Thomas told the king that early in 1537 Robert Tempest, a member of the Drapers' Company, 'hither conveyed away the said Ferdinando into Flanders ….. by a forged and surmised letter in your said subjects' name unto one George Constantine that had the oversight of the said Ferdinando unto your subjects' great discomfort and against all nature and the laws of your realm. Wherefore it may please your highness, in consideration your said subject hath left all his goods beyond sea and is a man not able to follow the law, that the said Robert Tempest, being sent for by pursuivant, may be commanded by your majesty to restore your said subjects' son and such recompense as by their wisdom shall be thought convenient'.

Presumably Tempest had been asked to execute this plan by Anna who wanted her young son back. In addition she had apparently given the younger son Robert into the care of another draper, John Chester, and Poyntz also asked the king to arrange for that boy to be found.

The letter concludes with a comment on his wife 'who hath continued in Antwerp ever since the said Banishment and refuseth to come hither unto her lawful husband with his goods and children, although divers ways and means hath been made unto her by your said subject'. This sounds as if Thomas had specific plans for his family, the details of which are unfortunately lacking.

In the following January all of the four children were naturalised as English citizens by act of parliament. However, there is no indication that any of them were actually in the country. [73]

Thomas had now been back in England for some years and his situation was not being resolved. He was apart from his family and his business interests. It would seem that he became very frustrated and decided upon direct action, rather as he had done in writing to his brother in the summer of 1535. He returned to the Low Countries.

iii. Brought unto Misery

... contrary to all his friends' counsel, gone up and about his business, openly in sight of the world as well in Antwerp, as in other places of this country.

Nicholas Wotton & Edward Carne to the Council 1544

What happened next can be partially discovered from two letters written to the Privy Council in London by Nicholas Wotton, England's ambassador in Brussels.

The first of these is dated December 1544. It is in reply to a letter from the Council in London. It seems that the Council had been approached by friends of Poyntz for help on his behalf. [74]

Poyntz must have arrived back in the Antwerp area no later than the autumn of 1543 because Wotton mentioned the efforts made on his behalf by the previous ambassador, Sir Francis Bryan, who left the post towards the end of that year. Initially there does not seem to have been any attempt to arrest him. The main concern was to get him to settle his debts, in particular as regards the guard from whose custody he had broken out seven years earlier. The guard no doubt expected Poyntz to reimburse the fine which had been imposed on him, but in addition money was probably owed for his board and lodging during the months of his imprisonment. Foxe recorded difficulties about payments at the time of his imprisonment.

Wotton's letter gives the impression of some frustration both with the authorities in Brussels and with Poyntz himself. The authorities seemed to waver over whether the matter could be settled easily or not. At first it appeared that if Poyntz sorted himself with the guard and presented himself at the prison there would be a pardon. However, later one official had 'forgotten' all that was agreed. The matter does not seem to have been helped by the fact that Poyntz, far from hurrying to comply with the demands made to settle the matter, was travelling around carrying on business, something against which his friends had advised him. No doubt he was anxious to try and produce some income for himself and his family.

Unfortunately the guard was not prepared to wait for ever. He arranged for Poyntz to be arrested in the street and placed in prison in Brussels.

Still Wotton endeavoured to settle things, having further discussions with local officials. However there now seems to have arisen another issue 'because of this business of the heretics that of late hath been detected in Antwerp, the which hath much exasperated the Emperor and his council'. It appears that the matter of heresy was now brought into the case based upon something that Poyntz was supposed to have said, possibly when in England. Poyntz denied the accusation but Wotton was told that a confession and witness statements existed. However even he was not able to gain access to these supposed documents. Also there was argument as to whether something that may have happened in England was any concern of the authorities in Brussels.[75]

To make matters worse the guard, seeing that Poyntz was now in prison and would surely be anxious to be out, was demanding more money, and interest also. He became even more adamant about sticking to his demands after Poyntz used strong words in argument with him. In addition Anna Poyntz and friends, who had apparently offered financial help, were now less willing to provide as much money as previously. [76]

Having outlined all these matters to the Council, Wotton concluded his letter by summarising a discussion with the lawyer working for Poyntz. The lawyer felt that things should be left for a while until the clamour about heresy died down, and in the hope that after a time the guard would be anxious for some money and so tone down his demands. He suggested that Wotton could then approach the authorities again and re-open negotiations.

There is much happening here, and hinted at. However the only further information seems to be in a letter to the Council of April 1545 in which Wotton briefly mentioned Poyntz and seemed to imply that a resolution was at hand. 'For Poyntz he hath promised to do the best he can to help to agree the matter with his adversary.' [77]

Later evidence suggests that the issue was concluded whilst Henry VIII still reigned. In Letters Patent Edward VI wrote of the matter being resolved by 'the earnest and often suits of certain special ministers of our late father'. This all implies that Poyntz left the Low Countries at some time between the late spring of 1545 and the end of 1546. [78]

These Letters Patent provide the only evidence of his situation over the years following his return. Once again there is no information as to the detail of his daily life but according to this document his situation had gone from bad to worse.

It is an unusual document. Letters Patent were documents issued by the monarch, usually for such actions as making appointments, giving rewards for services rendered, resolving disputes, and granting pardons. This document is a royal plea for assistance to be given to this man. 'Pitying the case of this man brought unto misery for so godly a cause we have thought good not only to prosecute him with our own grace and favour but also have thought good by these presents to recommend the miserable case of this poor man to all such our most loving subjects .. as may be induced to contribute towards the relief of the said Poyntz.' The king appealed to charitable bodies to assist him and his creditors to be generous.

Edward stated that Poyntz owed one thousand pounds – 'as we be informed' – 'for which he is daily troubled and imprisoned here'. This was a huge sum for those days but this is the amount quite clearly written in words in the document. This may have been a mixture of debts owed to people who had assisted in gaining his release from prison in Brussels, and others built up over the years in which he seems to have had little or no regular income. The reference to imprisonment must lead to the assumption that he was being thrown into one or other of the various debtors' prisons in London – the Fleet in the city, or the Marshalsea, the Clink, and the King's Bench in Southwark. Conditions of life could be very unpleasant unless a prisoner had money to pay for additional luxuries. It was common for wills of the period to leave money for bread for poor prisoners in these places and it is interesting to note that this was normal in the Shaa family.

The Letters explained that Poyntz was banished from the continent under pain of death. The reason the king gave for this situation was : 'certain things by him there attested and done of a good zeal to the advancement of God's true religion and glory and the relief of the true ministers thereof ….. and for no other cause'. [79]

These Letters Patent were issued in December 1551, the fifth year of Edward's reign. It is possible to see how the religious climate of this reign might encourage some to seek help for Thomas Poyntz but it is noteworthy that this took so long. It may or may not be relevant that the Letters were issued in the weeks between the trial and execution of the Duke of Somerset. The Letters read as if this is very much the king's own action and it must be possible that the fourteen year old king had somehow become aware of this man and his situation and felt a desire to do something for him. Alternatively it may be that some person or persons brought the case forward, but who?

On the Council were some who may have known of Poyntz's plight and taken an interest in him – the Essex neighbour of the Poyntz family Sir Wlliam Petre, Nicholas Wotton, now back in London, or Sir Thomas Cheyney, treasurer of the royal household. When the king wrote of having helped personally he may have meant by a donation from a fund for the poor to which he made a contribution on Sundays and Holy Days. This was part of the privy purse accounts and these were managed principally at this time by two men from Essex, Lord Darcy of Chiche, the Lord Chamberlain, and Sir John Gates, Vice Chamberlain. Gates had a house not far from the Poyntz's estate at North Ockendon as keeper of the south gate of Havering Park. Some believe that he had a great influence over Edward, who had spent part of his childhood at Havering, but this is disputed. He was known for his sympathies to the new religion. He was executed in 1553 after supporting the claim of Lady Jane Grey and, in his confession on the scaffold, he admitted to having been a great reader of the Bible. [80]

As at the time of Thomas Poyntz's arrival in London when a young man and as at the time of his writing to his brother in 1535, it is possible to identify a number of influential contacts he may have had but it is impossible to know to whom he did look for help and who did actually come to his aid. The only record of his being assisted as a result of the Letters Patent appears to be the 20s awarded to him by his own company, the Grocers', given on condition that he never asked again. The Acts of Court for this period are missing and so the detailed reasoning behind this decision is unknown. If Poyntz did owe one thousand pounds this contribution would do little to help! [81]

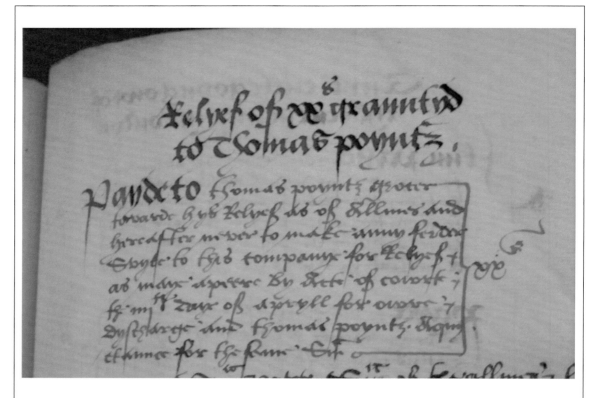

Grocers' Company Wardens' Accounts. In modern spelling this reads :

Relief of 20s granted to Thomas Poyntz.

Paid to Thomas Poyntz grocer rowards his relief as of alms and hereafter never to make any further suit to the company for relief as may appear by the Act of Court the fourth day of April for our discharge and Thomas Poyntz acquittance for the same.

Reproduced by permission of the Worshipful Company of Grocers' and the City of London, London Metropolitan Archives (CLC/L/GH/D/001/MS11571/005).

A search of the surviving accounts of city churches and other livery companies failed to find any further reference to him. However, many such accounts simply listed total amounts given to the poor in a particular period and so it is possible that he may have been helped without his specific details being recorded.

Whilst Thomas was enduring all these difficulties, now almost two decades since first leaving Antwerp, it seems possible that his wife was having the better time. A glimpse of Anna is obtained by a reading of the will of Robert Tempest made in August 1550 and supplemented in the following April. It is a very full will and the sums bequeathed to individuals, educational and charitable causes suggest that he was a wealthy man. From this will the impression is gained that Anna was still hosting merchants, probably in the same house in which she had lived and worked with Thomas. Her links with

Robert Tempest must have been close for he made bequests both to her and to three of the children (Ferdinando, Robert, and Susannah). There are also references which seem to imply that he and Anna had shared in some business dealings, possibly relating to land. These clues may explain why she was reluctant to leave her home in Antwerp to join Thomas and share an uncertain future in a strange country.

5. THOMAS POYNTZ IN ESSEX AND IN LONDON

i. Return to North Ockendon

... know ye that Thomas Poynes of Northockendon in the said countie esquir is assessyd w'in the said hundred of Chafforde wherein he doth dwell.

Certificate of residence for tax purposes 1556

On the death of John Poyntz in 1547 his wife, Anne, had inherited a lifetime interest in the estates at North Ockendon and elsewhere in Essex, together with the right of presentation to the living of North Ockendon. John insisted that if Thomas, or his sons, interfered with Anne's rights they would lose their future inheritance. Perhaps he thought that Thomas might try and obtain these lands to sort out his own problems. [82]

As was noted earlier, Anne died in 1554 and was buried in the church of St. Dunstan-in-the-West, Fleet Street, in the city of London.

The disposition of the family lands having been dealt with by John, the will of Anne was largely concerned with bequests to her grand-daughters by her first marriage of a considerable quantity of jewellery, including three pieces given her by Queen Mary. A £10 bequest to Gabriel was the only one to a member of the Poyntz family. [83]

By the term's of his brother's will Thomas now inherited the family estates which were centred on North Ockendon but also included the associated lands in the surrounding area. With North Ockendon he also inherited the advowson of the church and presented priests to the parish in 1556 and 1559. [84]

A certificate of residence granted for tax purposes confirms that he lived there and was to be taxed in Chafford Hundred rather than in London. [85]

Presumably the inheritance must have made things easier in a material sense. No details exist on these matters. Thomas' association with the affairs of the manor and its outlying parts is suggested by some records of manorial courts held in his name at South Ockendon and by part of a legal action brought against him by a woman called Jane Warren. She claimed that, 'with violence and strength', he had illegally entered into land in Upminster and North Ockendon of which she was the lawful tenant, had dispossessed her of her dwelling, and had taken deeds belonging to her. The one surviving document is that in which she put her case and so it is impossible to deduce the rights and wrongs of her allegation. [86]

One suggestion that things were looking up for Thomas was the admission of Gabriel and Robert to the Grocers' Company. They were 'received and sworn' in August 1554 on the basis of their father being a freeman of the company. This would seem to confirm that these two sons were both in England by then. Ferdinando was not admitted until 1557. [87]

ii. Telling the Story in Fleet Street

I Henry Bull … comend and resigne my self wholly into the handes of Jesus Christ the sonne of god my gracious lord and onely savior ~ assuredly trusting by faith in him to enherite and enioye everlastinge life in his glorious kingdom.

Will of Henry Bull 1577

When Thomas died in 1562 it was in London and, like his sister-in-law, he was buried at St. Dunstan-in-the-West. Apart from the family connection there it is just possible that he may have had some further interesting contacts in St. Dunstan's parish which would give additional reasons for him spending time that area. Amongst citizens of London who have been identified as supportive of the new religious ideas were two significant men who lived in the parish of St. Dunstan in the West, Henry Bull and Henry Elsing.

Henry Bull made his living as a physician based for many years in the parish of St. Dunstan's. Earlier in his life, when a student at Oxford, he had known John Foxe. When Foxe began to collect material together for his *Acts and Monuments*, more commonly known as *Foxe's Book of Martyrs*, it appears that Bull assisted in this collection and the subsequent editing. It has been suggested that Foxe and Bull would almost certainly have met to compare notes in late 1559 or early 1560 when both were in London. Brett Usher, who made this suggestion, considered that : 'Whenever it took place, the meeting will have provided a useful opportunity for checking out the recent doings and current whereabouts of a number of old friends and acquaintances'.[88]

The detail Foxe provides of the events surrounding, and subsequent to, the arrest of Tyndale, together with a specific statement in the 1570 edition, make it fairly certain that he was using the memories of Thomas Poyntz. However, there is no record of when, or to whom, Poyntz told his story. Conceivably he met either Bull or Foxe, or both, in St. Dunstan's parish.

Possibly here he met others also who would surely have been interested in talking with a man who a quarter of a century earlier had been so close to Tyndale in his last months of freedom. We have no account of the religious beliefs of Thomas Poyntz but the few clues we do have suggest that he was sympathetic to the reformers. The very fact that he was willing to take Tyndale into his house suggests this. In his letter to Cromwell he wrote of having suffered for the 'honour of God and the truth of his word', and in the letter written to his brother in 1535 he reckoned that the death of Tyndale would be a 'a great hindrance to the gospel'. [89]

One person whom he may well have known in that part of London, in addition to Bull, was Henry Elsing, baker of Fleet Street. He and Thomas Poyntz shared a common experience in that both had known a guest being arrested at their house who was later to be burnt. In 1535 William Tyndale had been taken from Thomas Poyntz's house, whilst in 1553 John Bradford was taken from the house of Henry Elsing in Fleet Street. Bradford was to spend two years in prison before being burned at the stake.

In Elizabeth's reign Elsing was closely connected with St. Dunstan's and his name, and his signature, appear several times in the Churchwardens' Accounts. Twice he was Churchwarden, the second time in the very year that Thomas Poyntz died so that their names face each other on the first two pages of the accounts for that year. [90]

Elsing was known as one who entertained men of reforming convictions, even in the dangerous days of Mary's reign. One of this group was Thomas Sampson. Elsing had stood surety for Thomas Sampson's first fruits – that is, the first year's income which was paid as a tax – when he became Rector of All Hallow's Bread Street. Sampson later wrote of John Bradford : 'Oftentimes have I sitten at dinner and supper with him, in the house of that godly harbourer of many preachers and servants of the Lord Jesus, I mean Master Elsyng..'. [91]

When Bradford lay in prison he wrote a letter of encouragement to Elsing whom he felt sure would soon himself be taken. He said that he had 'heard of the hazards' Elsing faced 'for the Gospel's sake' and he expected that the time of his 'suffering and probation' was at hand'. In fact Elsing was not taken then, or later, despite his hospitality to those now branded as heretics.[92]

Another who was to be burnt, John Philpot, wrote in a letter to a friend from his prison : 'Commend me to M. Elsing and his wyfe, and thanke them that they remembered to prouide me some ease in prison...' [93]

Whether Thomas Poyntz was part of a group who met in the Fleet Street area, in particular at the house of Henry Elsing, and whether this adds to the explanation for the place of his death and burial, there is no evidence to determine. It seems a plausible speculation but it can be no more. What is clear is that Poyntz and Elsing shared in common one thing at least – they had both given hospitality and encouragement to leaders of the new religious thinking, and they had done this at great risk to themselves and their families.

iii. Remembering Thomas Poyntz

For faithful service to his prince and ardent profession of the evangelical truth he suffered chains and imprisonment in regions across the seas.

Memorial tablet in North Ockendon church

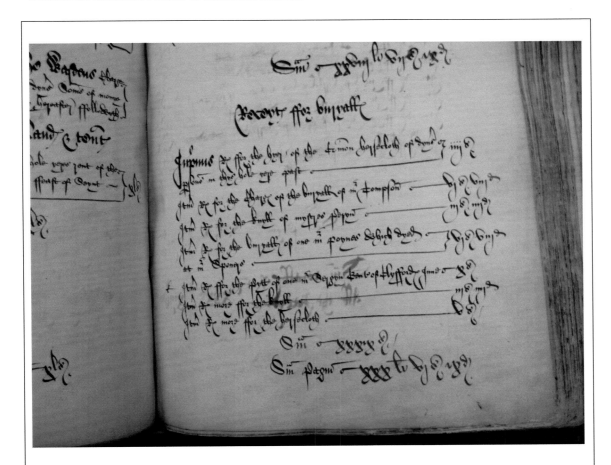

Churchwardens' Accounts St. Dunstan in the West. In modern spelling lines 5/6 read :

Item Received for the burial of one Mr Poynes which died at Mr Sponers 6s 8d.

Reproduced by permission of the City of London, London Metropolitan Archives (P69/DUN2/B/011/MS02968/001).

Who was Thomas Sponer?

Information about Thomas Sponer, at whose home Poyntz is recorded as having died, can be gleaned from a range of sources. [94]

He was apprenticed as a goldsmith in 1509 to John Mundy who, like Thomas Poyntz's father, had been an apprentice of Sir Edmund Shaa. It was no doubt Shaa who arranged the marriage of John Mundy to his granddaughter and the marriage of William Poyntz to his niece.

Sponer was made free of the Goldsmiths' Company in 1517, the very same year in which Thomas Poyntz was admitted to the Grocers'. He was presumably a practising goldsmith as in 1547 he was paid 15d to mend a chalice for St. Dunstan's. Ten years later he was Prime Warden of the Goldsmiths' Company.

Tax records show him living in St. Dunstan's parish by 1541. From 1551 to 1553 he was churchwarden. He appears several times in the account book over the years. From 1558 until his death in 1565 he supplied communion wine to the church, possibly as a sideline or through his son-in-law, John Hill, who was member of the Vintners' Company.

For at least three years Sponer was a representative of the Ward of Farringdon Without on the Common Council of the City of London. In his own immediate neighbourhood he is recorded as contributing to a collection in 1560 for the purchase of buckets and ladders against the eventuality of fire.

Thomas Sponer had a long standing contact with the Poyntz family. As far back as 1527 his name appears in the inquisition post mortem on the estates of William Poyntz, Thomas Poyntz's father.

It may be that their common links with the Goldsmiths' Company explain the origin of the friendship between Sponer and the Poyntz family. However, it is clear from the wills of John and Anne Poyntz, in both of which Thomas Sponer is appointed overseer, that the connection was, by that later date, more than just a friendship. Although not explicitly stated, the use of phrases 'my sister Sponer' by John and 'my brother Sponer' by Anne - phrases used in that period to describe a brother-in-law or sister-in-law - lead to the conclusion that Thomas Sponer's wife, Elizabeth, was Anne's sister. So it would appear that, out of long standing friendship and family ties, Thomas and Elizabeth Sponer may have given comfort to Anne and Thomas at the last and supervised their burial in their own parish church. [95]

Thomas Poyntz died on 5th May 1562 at the house of Thomas Sponer and was buried that day in the church of St. Dunstan in the West, close by where his sister-in-law had been buried eight years earlier.

The church stood slightly south of the present building, overlapping what is now Fleet Street. Being on the edge of the city, it later survived the Great Fire but was demolished to make way for road widening in the early nineteenth century. Outside the present church can be seen the statue of Queen Elizabeth I which does derives from her life time and which was set originally on Lud Gate. It was, of course, in her reign that Thomas Poyntz was brought to St. Dunstan's for burial.

The church register records the burial, and the Churchwardens' Accounts notes the payment of the burial fee. There is later a reference in the accounts to the 'covering' of his grave but there is no record of there ever having been an inscribed gravestone. As a result of the nineteenth century rebuilding of the church few older memorials remain. If there ever was a gravestone it would most likely have been lost at that time.[96]

It may be appropriate that Thomas Poyntz was laid to rest in St. Dunstan's for it appears that during William Tyndale's time in London he did preach in that church. Reference was made earlier to the merchant Humphrey Monmouth who made friends with Tyndale in London in 1523 and who supported him in various ways. When imprisoned in 1528, during one of Wolsey's heresy hunts, Monmouth made an answer to various charges laid against him. In the course of his answers he mentioned having heard Tyndale preach two or three times at St. Dunstan's and to having possessed some of Tyndale's sermon notes. The manuscript used first by John Foxe and, later, by John Strype in relating details of this letter is today in the British Library and clearly refers to St. Dunstan's in the West. [97]

Biographers of Tyndale have spoken warmly of the part played by Thomas Poyntz in the events surrounding Tyndale's arrest. On the five hundredth anniversary of Tyndale's birth David Daniell wrote of this time : 'The one person who can never be accused of dragging his feet, even at cost to his own liberty and fortune, was Thomas Poyntz'. Earlier in the twentieth century J.F.Mozley commented on the consequences of this commitment : 'In a wordly way his life was ruined by his generous championship of Tyndale : but the lustre of his deed is his perpetual possession'. [98]

In 1895 a limited edition book was published in London written by an historian of the Grocers' Company, John Abernathy Kingdon. He reviewed the lives of Thomas Poyntz and Richard Grafton, the latter a London printer

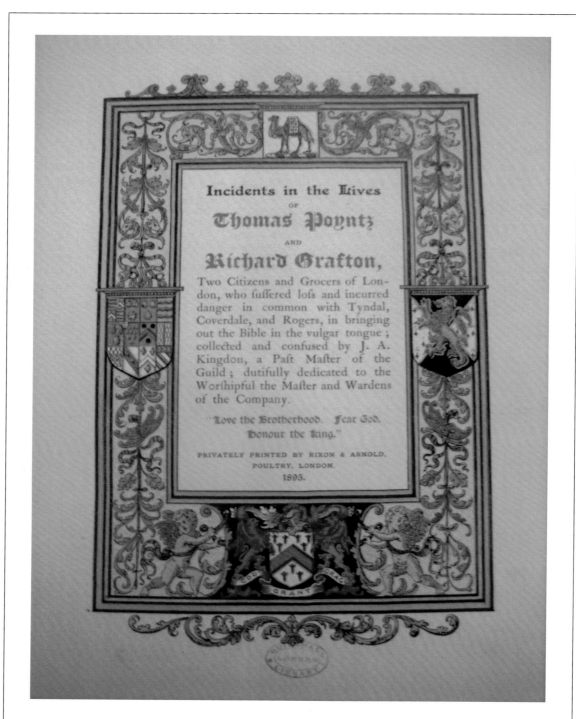

The title page of *Incidents in the life of Thomas Poyntz and Richard Grafton, two citizens and grocers of London, who suffered loss and incurred danger in common with Tyndal, Coverdale, and Rogers, in bringing out the Bible in the vulgar tongue* (London : Privately printed by Rixon & Arnold 1895) by J.A.Kingdon. Reproduced by permission of the City of London, Guildhall Library.

of that period whose output included early editions of the Bible in English.

Several key documents were reproduced in facsimile and transcription, including the letter of Thomas to John. The copy in London's Guildhall Library includes hand colouring which adds to an already fine production, making a worthy commemoration of these two men.[99]

Some years before this, in 1871, a major biography of Tyndale by Robert Demaus was published. Demaus commented of Poyntz that 'he had spared no pains, and he had shrunk from no peril' in his efforts to help. Demaus was careful to consult all original sources he could. It was his researchers in Belgium who discovered the document recording a fine on the guard from whose custody Poyntz escaped in 1536. [100]

Earlier still a history of the English Bible was written by Christopher Anderson. He was curious to see the memorials to Thomas Poyntz and his family in North Ockendon Church and described what he found there in the first year of Queen Victoria's reign.

'It was in the month of September 1837, or precisely three hundred years after the English Bible at which Tyndale laboured, the basis of all following editions, had reached this country. He found the little church, with its flint stone embattled tower covered with ivy, in a condition distinguished for its cleanliness; and the monuments of different families, some of them in elegant marble, in perfect preservation; but the humbler tablets excited the deepest interest. In horizontal lines …. are the monuments of the Poyntz family, in regular succession from about the middle of the fourteenth century; while that of Tyndale's friend remains, easily to be distinguished from the others.' Anderson read the inscription and noted the lack of any reference to Tyndale, without which, he commented, 'the lines themselves convey but feeble meaning'. He was concerned that in his time the work of Tyndale – 'perhaps the greatest benefactor that our native country ever enjoyed' – was far too little known and its importance too little understood.[101]

If Anderson were to visit St. Mary Magdalene's at North Ockendon today he would find it almost as he remembered. It still has the appearance of a village church set in the midst of fields, although the noise of traffic from the M25 is a reminder of changed times.

As he noted, the memorial to Thomas requires some background knowledge to understand as there is no mention of William Tyndale, in addition to which the Latin text and damaged lettering make it even harder for most people to read today.

Translated the inscription reads:

"Thomas Poyntz esquire, son of William Poyntz, at the death of his brother John became Lord of the Manor and Patron of the church. He married Anna van Calva daughter and co-heir of John Calva, native of Germany. They had sons Gabriel, Ferdinand and Robert and a daughter Susannah. For faithful service to his prince and ardent profession of the evangelical truth he suffered chains and imprisonment in regions across the seas plainly already destined to be killed except he himself trusting in divine providence looked for a miraculous escape from prison. Even now he sleeps in peace in this chapel. The year of our lord 1562, the fifth year of the reign of Queen Elizabeth."

There are two errors in this inscription. It is quite clear from the registers and accounts of the church of Saint Dunstan in the West, Fleet Street, that this is where Thomas was buried. Also, he died in the fourth regnal year of Elizabeth, not the fifth as stated on the memorial.

This tablet shows Thomas and Anna kneeling in prayer, facing each other over a two sided prayer desk. Thomas is dressed as a soldier, presumably as a recognition that as lord of the manor he might be required to raise troops in time of war. This tablet is one of a series of similar memorials to members of the Poyntz family, a scheme devised by Thomas's eldest son, Gabriel, and implemented around 1600. All the inscriptions are in Latin and quite damaged. [102]

In addition to the tablets the chapel has several other memorials to members of the Poyntz family from the fourteenth century onwards and it is dominated by a grand and colourful alabastar tomb with the recumbent effigies of Gabriel himself, and his wife Etheldreda.

On the five hundredth anniversary of Tyndale's birth in 1994 there were those who thought, as Anderson had done a century and a half before, that Tyndale's work was not recognised as it should be. Since then his immense contribution to the English Bible and the English language has been promoted through the Tyndale Society and, in particular, through its first Chairman, Professor David Daniell, who published a full study of Tyndale's life and work in 1994, has edited several books of his translations and writings, and has spoken endlessly around the world about the significance of his work. In 2004 Professor Daniell spoke at a Study Day organised by the Tyndale Society at North Ockendon which drew attention to Thomas Poyntz and his part in the Tyndale story.

Inevitably greater attention focused on Tyndale also draws attention to those around him and amongst these must be numbered Thomas Poyntz. Unlike

The memorial tablet to Thomas and Anna in St. Mary Magdalene Church, North Ockendon, Essex. Reproduced by permission of the Essex Record Office from its copy of *The Ancient Sepulchral Monuments of Essex* by Frederick Chancellor (1890).

some of those who were close to Tyndale, he was no scholar of Hebrew or Greek, he was no theologian, and he did not burn at the stake. However, he was a man with a clear sense of duty – to God, to his king, to Tyndale his guest, and to his family. He was willing to take active steps in situations where others might have kept a lower profile. He deserves an honoured niche in the story of the English Reformation.

iv. The Next Generation

Gabriel, himself, was dedicated to his enthusiasm for finding good literature.

From inscription on Gabriel's tomb at North Ockendon.

History does not record whether William Tyndale had any skills as a baby sitter. If he did he may well have been called upon when in the Poyntz household where the four children must have been born in fairly quick succession from around 1532.

After a long separation from their father the children did eventually settle in England some years after their naturalisation in 1542 and their later life appears to have been quite succesful despite the early upsets.

Gabriel was clearly the eldest son, probably born in 1532, with Ferdinando and Robert following. Where Susannah came in the family is unknown.

Shortly after Gabriel was admitted to the freedom of the Grocers' Company in the summer of 1544 a Gabriel Poyntz is recorded as matriculating at Basel University, at a time when many Englishmen of reformed sympathies were leaving for continental towns and universities in escape from the Marian regime and to prepare for better days. There can be no certainty that this was Thomas' son but it seems probable. Not least, the inscription on Gabriel's tomb at North Ockendon suggests that he had literary interests. It is interesting to note that in the Shakespeare Folger Library in Washington is a copy of *Of the Knowledge Which Maketh a Man Wise*, by the diplomat and humanist scholar Sir Thomas Elyot, on the title page of which is written : 'Gabriel Poyntz his book'. [103]

Under the terms of the will of his grandfather, John Poyntz, Gabriel did inherit the family estates on the death of his father in May 1562. Seven years later he married Etheldreda or Audrey Latham, widow of a Ralph Latham. She herself came from Arkesden, in north west Essex, but had lived with her

Gabriel Poyntz c1569 age 36.

Oil on panel.

Attributed to the Master of the Countess of Warwick.

Reproduced by permission of Christies' Images and Bridgeman Art Library.

first husband in North Ockendon. Ralph's will indicates that, like Gabriel, he held land in several parishes around that part of Essex. There is no mention of Gabriel in the will. [104]

Gabriel took an active part in Essex affairs, as his uncle, John, had done and as was expected of a man in his position. He achieved greater heights than John, serving two terms as sheriff of Essex and being knighted. A number of documents survive in the Essex Record Office showing him as exercising this authority, then a key post in the judicial system of the county.

At some point Gabriel acquired from Sir Thomas Heneage the property at Bevis Marks in the City of London which had once been the town house of the Abbots of Bury St Edmunds. It was a descendant, Sir Thomas Poyntz Littleton, speaker of the House of Commons and treasurer of the navy, who leased this site in 1699 for the building of the fine Spanish and Portuguese synagogue which still stands today, one of the hidden treasures of the city.

Gabriel died in 1607 and was buried in the church of St. Mary Magdalene at North Ockendon where he had prepared a magnificent alabaster memorial following the death of his wife who pre-deceased him in 1594. Gabriel and Etheldreda are represented in recumbent pose, their hands together as in prayer, Gabriel in armour and his wife in long gown and under-garment, both embroidered, with a high collar and ruff. The whole is surmounted by a tester with colourful decoration representing the heavens, with sun, moon, stars and clouds. This is by far the grandest of the memorials in the Poyntz's chapel.

Unlike Gabriel, whose name does not appear in records of the Grocers' Company after his admission, his two brothers, Ferdinando and Robert, whilst not appearing in records for some years after their admission, regularly paid their Brotherhood Money from the late fifteen sixties. [105]

Around ten years after his 1557 admission to the Grocers' Company there is a clue that Ferdinando was engaging in trade. London port records show him importing 'Levant taffeta'. About the same time he acquired from the company property in Mincing Lane with a condition that he built a 'fair gatehouse of stone' with the arms of the Grocers' Company above it, a requirement over which there was a later dispute. [106]

Ferdinando may have been the same as one of this name who is recorded in the 1580s as involved in work on the harbour at Dover and other public duties. [107]

The impression gained is of some success in public life. Sadly his personal life may have been less happy. The registers of the church of St. Dunstan in the East showing a Ferdinando Poyntz as having six children, five of whom died in infancy in 1576 and 1577. He himself died in 1586. There is no record of his burial at St. Dunstan's, although a 'Mrs Poynes' was buried there in 1588. [108]

Although the youngest brother, Robert, is recorded paying his Brotherhood Money to the Grocers' little else about him has come to light. A Robert Poyntz was buried at the church of St. Clement Dane in 1586.

The one girl in the family, Susannah, married a Richard Saltonstall. Richard came from Yorkshire and was a relative of the Saltonstalls who were amongst the earliest colonisers of America. Susannah had very probably first met him whilst still in Antwerp as he was active in trade with the continent, in due course becoming a leading exporter of cloth to the Low Countries. His own company was the Skinners', of which he was master on four occasions. He was to rise in city affairs as customer of the port of London, member of parliament for the city, and as an alderman, sheriff, and mayor in 1597. He was knighted in 1598.

Image of Susannah Saltonstall from the memorial in the church of St. Nicholas, South Ockendon, Essex.   © Brian Edwards

In 1576 Richard purchased the Manor of Groves in South Ockendon close to the manor of North Ockendon now held by his brother-in-law, Gabriel. Richard and Susannah were both buried in the church of St. Nicholas in South Ockendon. They are commemorated by a grand monument which Susannah devised after her husband's death in 1601 and which shows the couple kneeling and facing each other. Susannah lived on until 1613. Interestingly, the register of the burial at South Ockendon describes her as of the parish of St. Dunstan in the East, the same which is associated with Ferdinando, and the Grocers' Company records show Richard renting a property in Mincing Lane, the same lane in which Ferdinando acquired property from the company. [109]

Whilst records relate a fair amount of information about the children of Thomas Poyntz there are intriguing questions around which we can only speculate.

As both Gabriel and Susannah each commissioned their memorial during their lifetime it seems reasonable to suppose that the images represent true likenesses. Do these likenesses reflect those of their parents?

The children seem to have remained in close physical proximity in England. Does this reflect a close family unit in Antwerp and support they gave each other during the time after their father disappeared, a man of whom they must have had few childhood memories?

Finally, is it just possible that the older children may have had some vague recollection of a guest in their childhood home who spent his days with his head in books and papers, reading and writing, and who one day went out for lunch and was never seen again?

6. A POSTSCRIPT : WHO KILLED WILLIAM TYNDALE?

Obviously the simple answer to this question is that he was strangled and burnt as a heretic by the judicial authorities in Brussels. However, to read most biographies of William Tyndale is to gain the impression that this execution was largely brought about by Henry Phillips, an English student at Leuven University, acting as agent of some person or persons from amongst the ranks of the religiously conservative back in England. This explanation seems to be based primarily on the assertion by the chronicler Edward Hall that Phillips acted 'as many said, not without the help and procurement of some bishops of this realm'. [110]

The result of following this line has been that successive scholars over the past two centuries have engaged in finger pointing exercises at various known haters and hunters of heretics. At the same time not one of these writers has claimed to produce specific evidence to convict any of these persons of hatching a plot specifically against Robert Barnes, George Joye and William Tyndale, all three of whom Phillip's claimed to be pursuing, or even of having any communication with Henry Phillips.

In 1845 Christopher Anderson wrote at length about William Tyndale in his book *The Annals of the English Bible.* Having quoted Edward Hall he immediately went on to point an accusing finger at Stephen Gardiner, bishop of Winchester, noting that Phillips had been brought up at Poole, on the edge of Gardiner's diocese. He was sure that Gardiner was 'deeply concerned' in the intrigue 'but *if so,* he may have been the *chief,* for such was the well known temper of the man'. Anderson's choice of Gardiner was largely based on his conservative reputation. Anderson reminded his readers of how Tyndale's translation of the New Testament had been collected up and burnt by the bishops and now, he claimed, some of these bishops 'were still more eager to consign the translator himself to the flames'.[111]

Anderson's theory was addressed some quarter of a century later by Robert Demaus in *William Tyndale A Biography.* Demaus agreed that Gardiner was a possibility but he was far more cautious than Anderson. He pointed out that, apart from the 'vague assertion' of Edward Hall, 'not the smallest tittle of evidence has ever yet been adduced' against Gardiner in this matter. He went on to comment that, though many bishops would no doubt like to have seen Tyndale burn, 'if they were concerned in the plot, they have certainly shown wonderful skill in obliterating all traces of their participation in it'. [112]

When J.F.Mozley came to write his biography of Tyndale in 1937 he also sought to point the finger of blame at a bishop, again quoting Hall's words. He mentioned, without discussion, Gardiner, and Longland of Lincoln, but he himself felt the most likely candidate was John Stokesley, bishop of London. He remarked upon Stokesley's involvement in the pursuit of heresy and his deathbed claim as to the number of heretics he had helped to convict. He made reference to two servants of Stokesley seen in Antwerp in 1533. 'All this', he suggested, 'makes it reasonable enough to see in him the chief backer, if not the prime engineer, of the plot which destroyed Tyndale'. However, Mozley did add the crucial words 'But yet we cannot say that this is certain'.[113]

David Daniell, whilst quoting Mozley in his *William Tyndale a Biography* (1994), cautiously prefaced his next paragraph with the words 'If this is correct..'. He offered no other names. [114]

So the leading Tyndalian scholars of the nineteenth and twentieth centuries each sought to name a bishop in line with Edward Hall's statement – although, in fact, Hall had written of 'some bishops', not simply one. In addition Hall had made clear that he was passing on current gossip, 'as many said'. There is no indication as to whether this gossip was mere speculation or whether there was any firmer information being passed around. Demaus was surely right when he described this as a 'vague assertion'. The end result of this theorising on the basis of Hall was to suggest that some unidentified bishop of England and a young student, Henry Phillips, were the actors in a two man drama that brought about the death of William Tyndale, and also sought the fall of Robert Barnes and George Joye.

We may wonder whether it is really plausible that a leading bishop (anxious to preserve his own position and life amidst the religious uncertainties of Henry VIII's England) would dream up a plan to remove three notable English reformers - one of whom, Robert Barnes, was being used in diplomatic missions – look around for a likely accomplice, chance upon an impoverished student who had fallen out with his father over his poor stewardship of money and whose devious ways were several times detected by others, present him with a bag of gold, send him off to study at Leuven, and at the same time trust him to use some of the money to obtain an arrest warrant from the imperial authorities for the three English heretics and then be sure that they were brought to the flames!

Widening the Possibilities

With the dawn of the twenty first century an attempt was made at a different approach. Brian Moynahan, in his book *If God Spare My Life : William Tyndale, the English Bible and Sir Thomas More – A Story of Martyrdom and Betrayal* (2002), recognised issues with what had become the traditional view and saw that there might be other possibilities. He still homed in on one person but in this case not a bishop, instead a layman, Sir Thomas More. [115]

Those sympathetic to the new religious ideas infiltrating England in the second quarter of the sixteenth century knew to be afraid of Lord Chancellor More. Lurid tales circulated as to his treatment of those interrogated at his Chelsea home. More, the man who seemed to delight in burning heretics, and More the scholar, had combined in a memorable written debate with Tyndale. Thus to consider him a candidate for Phillip's master seems, at least at first sight, a reasonable suggestion. Moynahan also pointed out known links between More and English religious refugees in the Low Countries, and also the favour in which More was held by the ruler of those lands and Holy Roman Emperor, Charles V. Charles was nephew of Catherine of Aragon, she who had so recently been offloaded by Henry VIII, and he had expressed appreciation of More's efforts on behalf of his aunt.

Whether or not Moynahan's theorising is accepted it did at least have value in widening the discussion. Apart from introducing a new suspect from outside the episcopate, Moynahan usefully reminded his readers of the presence in the Low Countries of a group of religious exiles from Henry VIII's England and he raised the very important question as to who had sufficient influence to persuade the authorities in Brussels to prosecute a case against the three Englishmen.

The one obvious objection to the involvement of More is that he was already in the Tower some months before Phillips is first recorded at Leuven in a matriculation record of December 1534. More was to remain in those grim precincts until his execution in July 1535 but Moynahan argued that he was in contact with friends outside during this time and through them he could have commissioned Phillips.

It might be argued that More had little to lose by involving himself in such a scheme and that through his contacts both in London and Antwerp the actions of Phillips could be monitored. However, if More was the guide and paymaster of this scheme why should Phillips have continued to pursue it even when everybody must have known that the former Lord Chancellor was dead? Four months after More's execution Phillips was thrown into panic when he heard that Tyndale might be released into the hands of Thomas Poyntz and so he managed to negotiate the arrest of the one man who seems to have been constantly active on Tyndale's behalf.

When Thomas Poyntz had written to his brother about the cause of Tyndale in the previous August he had pinned the blame on 'the papists'. Whilst his letter was highly critical of the English bishops he had not specifically pointed in their direction as regards Tyndale's arrest. He had been in Antwerp for some years and would have picked up news and gossip within the merchant community. Phillips had dined in his house and they had talked at length on at least one occasion on which, as Poyntz later realised, he was being sounded out as a possible ally in some scheme. Yet Poyntz says nothing more specific than 'the papists' when writing of the plotters. This may have been simple discretion or perhaps he genuinely knew nothing. [116]

The Papists in England and in Exile

When Poyntz wrote of 'the papists' he could have had in mind the high profile characters who have already been noted as suspects, the conservative bishops in England or Sir Thomas More. Alternatively he may also have been thinking more widely, aware, as he undoubtedly was, of lesser, but still significant, figures in England and their links with religiously conservative exiles in the Low Countries.

Moynahan drew attention to some of those who were known or suspected of links with Thomas More. One of the most interesting, and moving regularly between England and the Continent, was Anthony Bonvisi. Born in England of an old Italian family he was a merchant of great wealth. As the English Reformation unfolded Bonvisi became known as a defender of those who adhered to the old faith and yet managed to retain a position within English society. By virtue of his wealth and constant travelling he was often able to serve the crown in matters both financial and diplomatic. By the time of the events surrounding Tyndale's arrest he was probably about sixty years of age and throughout his adult life he had been a close friend of Thomas More. In Edward's reign he settled in Leuven where his house was known as a centre of comfort for the exile English community and where he died in 1558.

English diplomats and spies regarded Bonvisi with suspicion. He was known to have been an intermediary between More and exiles abroad. He was particularly reckoned to be giving succour to William Peto and Henry Elstow. These two men were leading figures in the Observant Franciscan order who had fled to Antwerp in 1533 after Peto had preached against Henry's divorce and that in the presence of the king himself.

Another significant figure from this period was Robert Buckenham, former prior of the Dominican Convent in Cambridge. His arrival in Leuven was about the time of Tyndale's arrest. He was said to be associating with Phillips and he is generally reckoned to have been involved in preparing the case against Tyndale prior to his trial. [117]

A few other names are recorded from this period and there may well have been some of which no record remains. Leuven was a known centre for English dissidents and diplomats seem to have looked upon the English students there with suspicion. They saw the cloak of study as often but a cover for intrigue.

As time passed the religious position of these exiles became increasingly clear by their association with Reginald Pole. By birth he was a member of the Yorkist dynasty and seen by Henry as an increasing threat after writing a forceful work including material on the divorce and the English church. Increasingly plans were laid to silence Pole but with no success. When the campaign against Pole and his contacts reached its climax in 1539 with the *Act of Attainder against the Marquess of Exeter and others* the names of several of the English exiles were included, as was that of Henry Phillips. His naming was unconnected with the Tyndale affair but rather that he had declared 'that venemous serpent the Bishop of Rome to be supreme head of the church' in England. [118]

As with the great, so with the lesser, there is nothing in all the accounts or diplomatic correspondence which associates any of these characters with Henry Phillips in his activities which led to Tyndale's arrest, or later that of Poyntz. At the same time he would certainly have known some of them and by early 1536 Henry VIII was sending out messages across Europe seeking the arrest of Phillips who seems to have been already associated in the official English mind with other characters of concern. It was not particularly, if at all, what had happened to Tyndale which bothered Henry, but rather a suspicion that these exiles were engaged in treasonous plotting. Whether such plotting included bringing about harm to the likes of Barnes, Joye and Tyndale, is quite unknown but it must be a possibility that Phillips was acting within a wider group which may have had links with high places in England but which also included exiles abroad. He was the front man in the arrest of both Tyndale and Poyntz, thus the one identified for posterity by John Foxe.

Gabriel Donne 'the crafty assistant'

Only once is there a suggestion in written records that Phillips had an accomplice. This is in a letter of Thomas Theobald to Thomas Cranmer in July 1535 when the writer recorded a conversation with Phillips in which he claimed that only one person was 'of his counsel' and that was Gabriel Donne. Donne was a monk who had studied at Oxford and then at Leuven from 1530. He was somewhat older than Phillips and, shortly after Tyndale's arrest, returned to England as the last abbot of Buckfast in Devon. He was later to serve as a secular priest in London and would eventually be buried before the high altar of Old St. Paul's. [119]

In 1845 Christopher Anderson vilified Donne as Phillips' 'crafty assistant' and as having a 'degraded character' and noted with surprise 'it must appear passing strange that he should have escaped the searching enquiries not only of Foxe and Strype, but of all later historians'. When Robert Demaus came to write of these events some years later he described Donne as 'this traitorous friar'. Both of these writers assumed that Donne's appointment to Buckfast was a reward for his part in the plot, a reward made by an innocent Thomas Cromwell at the instigation of the powerful in England who had initiated and financed the scheme. [120]

When J.F. Mozley wrote in 1937 he was much less sure about any guilt attaching to Donne, beyond possibly knowing something of Phillip's actions, and he dismissed the idea of the post at Buckfast being a reward. [121]

Theobald's letter is the only mention of Donne and is based solely on the word of Henry Phillips, a man several times caught out speaking untruths. On the other hand there is no obvious reason why Phillips should have mentioned this name unless it were true. Unlike, for example, his claim in Rome to have been related to Thomas More, the mention of Donne would not benefit him in any obvious way.

Perhaps Mozley was nearest the truth when he suggested that Donne merely knew something of the plot. If he had been actively involved surely he would have stayed around to see the matter through. To return to England almost immediately after Tyndale's arrest would seem rather irresponsible. As to the appointment to Buckfast, there is no clue in official records as to anybody but Thomas Cromwell being involved. Murky though is often the world of politics and diplomacy it seems unlikely that the scheme against Barnes, Joye and Tyndale was in any way the project of Thomas Cromwell, not least at a time when Barnes was involved in diplomatic missions between England and the Lutherans states. Surviving correspondence of this period often features pleas to Cromwell for positions either for the writer or his friends. No such correspondence exists seeking a favour on behalf of Donne.

A Radicalised Young Man?

In Mozley's discussion of Gabriel Donne he pointed out that 'Phillips ever describes himself as the chief actor, and so is described by all his enemies'. As has already been outlined, there were those in England and on the Continent unhappy with the way events were flowing at home who would wish to see the likes of Barnes, Joye and Tyndale removed and some of whom might have been willing to engage in a scheme to this end. In such a device Phillips might have been the local man on the ground, 'the chief actor'. However, at the same time, without new evidence coming to light, there is absolutely no way of being sure that this happened. Demaus was certainly correct when he wrote that, if some bishops were involved, they had covered their tracks brilliantly and the same must be said of More or any other figure or group. [122]

As an alternative proposal, is it just conceivable that there was no such behind the scenes figure or group and that Henry Phillips acted alone in this matter and that he was not 'the chief actor' but the sole actor? This is certainly the impression gained from John Foxe's account and from various references in diplomatic correspondence.

Perhaps today this idea of a young man, studying in a foreign university, being led to an extreme religious viewpoint which will lead him to conceive and attempt to execute a plan to bring harm to those he considers enemies of God, may not seen so unlikely as it might have done some years ago.

However, to accept such a version of events requires assuming that Phillips had been radicalised within the conservative religious community, that he had personal financial resources to get himself established at Leuven and to execute a plan to remove three leading English 'heretics', and that he was able to persuade the authorities in Brussels to issue him with a 'commission' to bring about these arrests.

Letters Home

Until Henry Phillips arrived at Leuven, and then began scheming in Antwerp and Brussels, there is no indication of his religious viewpoint. His own father's will, written in the reign of Philip and Mary, certainly does not suggest a man of conservative religious view. He commended his 'simple soul' to God, seeking forgiveness of his sins, and requesting no 'funeral pomp'. Richard Phillips was well established in Dorset, serving as a member of parliament and sheriff and having oversight of the customs arrangements in Poole. Whilst Henry was pursuing his scheming during 1536, his brother Thomas was seemingly in some trouble from which the influence of Thomas Cromwell was required to extricate him. In due time Thomas' son, Edward, was to become speaker of the House of Commons and builder of Montacute House in Somerset, and was well known as a prosecutor of resistance. This was certainly not a family tainted by suspicion of religious conservatism or treasonous plotting. [123]

However, the fact that Phillips became part of the Leuven community may suggest that he had already moved to a conservative viewpoint whilst in England. If so, when, where and by whom he was so influenced is quite unrecorded. From pleading letters he wrote, probably in late 1536 or in the following months, there are two interesting names which appear from his time in England, a Thomas Brerewood and a Dr. Underhill.

Phillips mentioned to his mother that he had written to Underhill but no letter survives. This may have been the John Underhill who was a prebend of the collegiate church of St. Stephen at Westminster and who also held a prebend in the diocese of Salisbury. Why Phillips wrote to him is unknown. The only obvious link is that Salisbury was his home diocese. [124]

As for Brerewood, much more certain information survives, together with two letters from Phillips, both written in Latin, one amongst the letters of 1536/7 and the other of 1538. [125]

After graduating BCL at Oxford Brerewood was ordained priest in London in 1516. It seems that he may have been based initially in the London diocese but by 1524 his interests were moving to Exeter, becoming archdeacon of Barnstaple in 1528 and chancellor to the bishop of Exeter.

As with Underhill, the connection between Henry Phillips and Thomas Brerewood is uncertain. However, if Phillips is to be believed, then it would appear that Brerewood was known to his parents, possibly having played some part in the boy's education.

The first letter was seemingly enclosed with one to Henry's brother Thomas with the request that it be passed on by hand. Henry referred to Brerewood as his 'only patron', pleading with him to assist a reconciliation with his parents 'for due to your merits my parents are obedient to you'. He sought only 'the memory of erring youth to be destroyed'. He invited Brerewood to send out to him a person he had educated and Phillips would 'be a servant to him, for I consider every type of man who knows literature honourable'. A year later Phillips wrote again. This time Christopher Joy, then in London, was asked to pass the letter on to Brerewood. Joy was another who had studied at Leuven and who was regarded dubiously by some in England. In this letter Phillips said that he had been upset as Brerewood seemed to have forgotten him but he had been assured by a mutual acquaintance that this was not so. He told Brerewood that he would be amazed to learn that he had been fighting in the imperial army. He again sought reconciliation with his father through Brerewood. He addressed the letter 'To the very dear and lord master Thomas Brerewood, the highest chancellor of the reverend bishop of Devon, his most worshipful patron'.

Even assuming that Brerewood had been involved in some stage of Phillips' education there is really nothing to suggest that either he, or John Underhill, would have been an influence towards an extreme conservative position. Both men seem to have had largely uneventful careers in the church. When in 1537 Lord Chancellor Audley sought the deanery of Exeter for Brerewood a note written by Thomas Cromwell said that he had done 'the king at all times good service'. It is interesting that, though Cromwell seemed disposed to this appointment, Henry VIII intervened and insisted on another candidate. Is it just possible that the king had seen the intercepted letters which may have linked Brerewood in his mind with Phillips? Sadly Brerewood spent the last couple of years of his life in the Tower but that is another story. [126]

The nine letters Phillips wrote to family and other contacts give no clue as to how he was influenced towards the attitudes which seem to have guided his actions in 1535. That he had become impassioned about the situation in England seems clear from a letter of Thomas Theobald to Thomas Cromwell only a few weeks after Tyndale's arrest which reported that 'He railed at Louvain and in the queen of Hungary's court most shamefully against our king his grace and others ..... rejoicing that he trusted to see the emperor to scourge his highness with his council and his friends'. [127]

Money Lost and Found

Even if motivated to extreme actions the question of his financing remains and has perplexed those who have addressed the issue. According to the letter already mentioned for his mother he had lost money entrusted to him by his father through a mixture of gambling and carelessness. If so he must have arrived in London penniless. Yet within a year or so at the most, and presumably without having further contact with his family, he is found a student at Leuven. He needed money to travel there and to sustain himself once arrived. It is also likely that he needed money for purposes of bribery in executing his scheme.

Knowing his tendency to untruthfulness it must be considered a possibility that he didn't lose the money but rather stole it and made his own way to Louvain. This seems to have been one version of events which circulated and, in the letters home, he appeared to believe that his father had initiated legal proceedings against him over the money issue.

To those who met him abroad it seemed that he was financially secure. One correspondent wrote to Cromwell that Phillips 'had more money than all the Englishmen that then were' at Leuven. According to John Foxe this was very much the impression gained by Thomas Poyntz. [128]

Another idea being rumoured was that Phillips had some personal income. Thomas Theobald, in the letter quoted earlier, commented 'either this Phillips hath great friends in England to maintain him here, or else, as he showed me, he is well beneficed in the bishopric of Exeter'. An earlier letter to Cromwell from a Robert Faryngton had a postscript 'I am credibly informed that Phillips had two benefices and a pretend when he went over the sea'. [129]

This was a time when laymen, even sometimes quite young boys, could acquire prebends and benefices from which they derived an income, paying something for a chaplain to perform priestly duties. As to whether this was the case with Phillips there seems no record to tell. Evidence appears completely lacking of his being ordained to any order of ministry or of his being appointed to any prebend or benefice. He himself made no such claims in his surviving correspondence. [130]

Again all this may have been but a fiction put about by Phillips to explain his having ready money. He may have mentioned Exeter as this was a diocese in which he had contact through Brerewood. Perhaps it should be noted that the Exeter diocese in pre-Reformation times, then including Cornwall, had a significant number of collegiate churches, each with several prebends.

It would seem that after the arrest of Tyndale his source of income dried up. When he wrote to his mother, possibly early in 1537, he claimed to have suffered 'penury and poverty' for two years. The main purpose of his writing the group of letters to his family and others at that time was to seek reconciliation in the hope that his parents would give him financial support allowing him to continue studying for a further three years. 'Then', he wrote to his mother, 'you shall see all things recompensed and your sorrow turned into joy'. He insisted that if his parents did not help 'necessity shall compel me for to go unto the wars or to be some serving man ..... contrary to my mind or profit'.

Apart from this uncertainty as to whether Phillips had some personal source of income there are at least two other objections to the idea that the project was essentially his alone. Again there is the puzzle as to how the authorities would have been persuaded to issue a commission for the arrest of Barnes, Joye and Tyndale. Surely it is unlikely that they would have done so at the insistence of a twenty year old student alone? Further, once Thomas Poyntz escaped from custody in the late winter of 1535/6 it seems that Phillips also fled the scene and spent the remainder of 1536 travelling in France, Germany and Italy. If this really was his scheme it seems surprising that he abandoned it in this way, except, of course, that by now Henry VIII had sent out a request for his arrest to the rulers of Europe.

A Local Affair?

Another possibility must be that the scheme was essentially a local affair with Phillips used as the bait to trap Tyndale.

Though Phillips absconded from the Low Countries by March of 1536 the authorities pursued the case against Tyndale to its end the following autumn. If Phillips had any leverage over them it was now gone and it must have been known that in England he was branded a traitor. Presumably if there was a lukewarm attitude to the matter it could have been dropped and either Tyndale simply left to rot in prison or in some way released. The fact that this did not happen suggests that either the pressure being brought to bear had a wider and more influential base than Phillips alone or that the authorities themselves were intent on pursuing the matter.

To suggest that the commission for the three arrests was essentially a local decision avoids the need for any explanation as to how any Englishman or group of Englishmen could bring the necessary pressure in Brussels. As to Phillips, it could be that the authorities looked to the group of English dissidents at Leuven for somebody to assist them. He could have been used to find out more about Tyndale's work and thoughts, as well as identifying his residence and he himself at the moment of arrest. The money he seemed to have at an early stage could have been bribes from Brussels rather than, as is generally assumed, money with which to pay out bribes.

Again, to follow this line does have to assume that Phillips had resources to get to Leuven in the first place and pay his living costs and costs of his servant. It also has to assume that the authorities who initiated the prosecution were prepared to risk upsetting the English merchant community.

Conclusion

In the plot to destroy Tyndale Phillips was clearly the front man but it seems impossible to be at all sure whether he was acting alone or, as seems more likely, with others and, if the latter, the identity of these. Without further evidence coming to light it may never be known who was really responsible for the killing of William Tyndale.

Early seventeenth century tester above the tomb of Sir Gabriel Poyntz in the church of St. Mary Magdalene, North Ockendon, Essex.

REFERENCES AND NOTES

BL British Library; ERO Essex Record Office; HRO Hereford Record Office; KH&LC Kent History & Library Centre; LPL Lambeth Palace Library; L&P Letters and Papers Foreign and Domestic of the Reign of Henry VIII ed. J.S.Brewer et al (London 1862-1932) (Most of the BL and TNA documents are summarised in these volumes at www.british-history.ac.uk); LMA London Metropolitan Archives; TNA The National Archives; ODNB Oxford Dictionary of National Biography 2004; VCH Victoria County History.

All references to Tyndale in *The Acts and Monuments* by John Foxe are from the relevant sections in *The Unabridged Acts and Monuments Online* or *TAMO* (1563 and 1570 editions) (HRI Online Publications, Sheffield, 2011). Available from http//www.johnfoxe.org.

References to *Letters and Papers Foreign and Domestic of the Reign of Henry VIII* mean that the original documents were not consulted.

[1] Sir J. Maclean *Historical and Genealogical Memoirs of the Family of Poyntz* (1886 New Edition Baltimore 1983) for genealogy of the various branches of the Poyntz family. *VCH Essex* Vol. 10 pp. 110 - 112 for descent of manor of North Ockendon.

[2] A.J.Prescott Essex Rebel Bands in London in W.H.Liddell & R.G.E. Wood *Essex and the Great Revolt* (Essex Record Office 1982) pp. 56, 88 & 89.

[3] Feet of Fines Essex Vol. III 1327 – 1422 (Colchester 1949) pp. 168/1721, 179/1845 & 180/1854 for land transactions. Register of Bishop Robert Braybrooke of London LMA DL/A/A/004/MS09531/003 f 117 for presentation to North Ockendon.

[4] VCH Essex Vol. 1 p.337. There are some records of this manor held amongst the muniments of Westminster Abbey.

[5] VCH Essex Vol. 7 pp.120 - 121 for Manor of Poyntz. ERO D/Dbe M13, M18, M19 & M20 for manorial records.

[6] TNA E150/310/2 Inquisition Post Mortem William Poyntz 1527 & C142/133/134 Inquisition Post Mortem Thomas Poyntz 1562 for fullest descriptions of land holdings. An Inquisition Post Mortem was an enquiry into the estates of a deceased person, in particular to determine the heir and any rights due to the crown. It was convened by the local escheator who assembled a jury to determine the facts.

[7] LPL Stafford 149v Will of John Poyntz 1447. TNA PROB11/5/107 Will of John Poyntz 1469. Calendar of Close Rolls Henry VII Vol. 1 1485 – 1509 Item 1095 1499 for sale of East Wickham.

[8] R. Newcourt *Repertorium Ecclesiasticum Parochiale Londinense* (1708-10) for presentation to North Ockendon. Goldsmiths' Company Court Minutes A p.193 for admission of William to his apprenticeship, p. 260 for admission to the Livery & pp. 266 & 274 for quarterage payments.

[9] For More's account see Richard Sylvester, ed. *The Complete Works of St. Thomas More, Volume 2: The History of King Richard III* (Yale University Press, New Haven and London 1963).

[10] TNA PROB11/8/187 for will of Edmund Shaa 1488. B. Varley *The History of Stockport Grammar School including the Life of Sir Edmond Shaa, Kt., P.C. Founder* (Manchester 1957). T.F. Reddaway *The Early History of the Goldsmiths' Company 1327-1509* with L.E.M. Walker ed. *The Book of Ordinances 1478-83* (London 1975). P. Tucker Edmund Shaa in *ODNB*.

[11] John A. Strype *A Survey of the Cities of London and Westminster* (London 1720) Volume II Book 5 Chapter 6 www.hrionline.ac.uk/strype. Philip Morant *History of Essex* (1768). TNA PROB 11/14/156 will of John Shaa 1504.

[12] A.H.Thomas & E.D.Thornley eds. *The Great Chronicle of London by Robert Fabyan* (London 1938) pp.290-326.

[13] J.P. Carley William Blount in *ODNB*. R.A.B. Mynors. & D.F.S. Thompson trans. The *Correspondence of Erasmus* (Toronto 1974). For Mountjoy as arbitrator ERO D/DQ 14/2. For the Book of Hours ERO T/B 105/1.

[14] F.G.Emmison *Tudor Secretary Sir William Petre at Court and at Home* (London 1961).

[15] Edmund and his daughter are mentioned both in the Inquisition Post Mortem of William TNA E150/310/2 1527 and in the will of John Poyntz TNA PROB11/31/546 1547. Also he is probably the Edmund mentioned with William in a document relating to the Isle of Sheppey TNA E41/309 1523. Henry, apart from being named on the memorial of c1600, may be the Henry named as a feoffee of the manor of East Sutton and other land KH&LC CKS - U120/T1/24/1 1528. William's admission to the Mercers after apprenticeship is recorded in the company's membership records.

[16] TNA C142/35/26 & E150/305/3 Inquisition Post Mortem Henry Patmore 1520. TNA PROB 11/20/40 will of Henry Patmore 1520. John A. Strype *A Survey of the Cities of London and Westminster* (London 1720) Volume I Book 2 Chapter 8 www.hrionline.ac.uk/strype for inscription.

[17] I am grateful to Andrew Hope who first drew my attention to Julian and who later clarified details of the Patmore family, making it seem likely that the Thomas in trouble in 1520 was a son of Julian (Letter from Andrew Hope in *The Tyndale Society Journal* No.39 Autumn 2010 pp. 54/55).

[18] TNA E150/310/2 Inquisition Post Mortem William Poyntz 1527. No will survives.

[19] TNA C/1/666/16 for John and Anne as man and wife. This chancery document is addressed to Thomas More as Lord Chancellor and so dates from the period 1529-1532.

[20] *VCH Buckinghamshire* Volume 3 (1925) pp. 20-31 for Isaac Sibley. TNA PROB11/22/359 for will of John Cheyney.

[21] Interestingly Wyatt addressed two poems to a John Poyntz. In view of the greater prominence of the Poyntz family of Gloucestershire these references are more probably to the John of Alderley in Gloucestershire, son of Sir Robert Poyntz, but, in view of the Kent connection, there is just the possibility that one may have been addressed to John of Ockendon. Also, in the Royal Collection, there is a drawing of a John Poyntz by Hans Holbein. Again, this is almost certainly of John of Alderley, one of whose descendants, the Earl of Harrowby, possesses a painting based upon it.

[22] BL Royal 17Bxviii Privy Purse Expenses of the Princess Mary for details of gifts to her. ERO D/DP/A12 & 13 Ingatestone Hall Provision Accounts for 1548 & 1552 in which Anne Poyntz is recorded as sending a present of two carp to Ingatestone in September 1548, and being entertained there in August 1552.

[23] TNA SP11/1/15 Coronation of Queen Mary 1553. LMA P69/DUN2/B/011/MS02968/001 Churchwardens' Accounts for receipt of burial fee and provision of a stone. There are no burial records until 1558. F. Madden Ed. *Collectanea Topographica et Genealogica* Volume IV 1837 for details of the stone. See p. 58 for information on Thomas Sponer.

[24] TNA E315/269 Book of Accounts of the Hospital of St. Thomas of Acre. D.J.Keene & V. Harding *Historical Gazetteer of London Before the Great Fire* (London : Centre for Metropolitan History 1987) St. Martin Pomary 95/17 pp. 184–186 where the site of the house is identified. This work states that Poyntz rented the property for two years and that it was then vacant until 1526 but the account book shows him renting through this period.

[25] LMA CLC/L/GH/D/001/MS11571/003 Grocers' Company Wardens' Accounts.

[26] LMA CLC/L/GH/D/001/MS11571/003 & 004 Grocers' Company Wardens' Accounts for payment of Brotherhood Money. TNA C1/482/25 Action by Thomas Poyntz re. almonds. TNA C1/556/40 action by Thomas Archer re. arbitration.

[27] TNA C82/567 Fiat for travel December 1525 (this is not recorded in L&P, although one is given for 1532 which two searches of the relevant boxes of original material failed to find : L&P XXI/2/773/ii/24).

[28] BL Cotton Galba Bx.60 August 1535 Letter of Thomas Poyntz to John Poyntz.

[29] Oskar De Smet *De Englese Natie te Antwerpen in de 16de eeuw* (Antwerp 1950-4). I am grateful to Dr. Paul Arblaster for drawing my attention to this book and for searching archives in Antwerp for any references to Thomas Poyntz.

[30] TNA PROB11/34/418 1551 Will of Robert Tempest which sheds some light on Anna at a later period..

[31] In TNA SP1/156/105 1539, a letter to Thomas Cromwell, Poyntz wrote that his eldest child (probably Gabriel, but possibly Susannah) was six years old. On a portrait of Gabriel dated 1569, painted around the time of his marriage, it is stated that he was thirty six years old (see p.65) Entry 1 in Christies Catalogue for a sale of Important British

Pictures 1990. The name of the second son is variously spelt Fernando or Ferdinando, Poyntz using the second spelling in his letter to Henry VIII TNA SP1/101/1231 1541.

[32] BL Cotton Galba Bx.60 August 1535 Letter of Thomas Poyntz to John Poyntz in which he gives the length of time Tyndale was at his house as three quarters of a year. At the end of this time Tyndale was arrested. Although there is some dispute about the date of the arrest it was in April or May 1535 and so the time of Tyndale's arrival is likely to have been mid to late summer of 1534.

[33] HRO AL19/12 Register of Richard Mayhew of Hereford for ordination as sub-deacon. LMA DL/A/A/005/MS09531/009 Register of Richard FitzJames of London for ordinations as deacon and priest. Andrew J. Brown *William Tyndale on Priests and Preachers* (Inscriptor Imprints London 1996) for transcriptions and translations from these registers and from those of Oxford University. Brian Edwards *Travel with William Tyndale* (Day One Publications, Leominster 2009) pp.22, 25 & 26 for photographs of London and Oxford registers. Andrew Hope Who was William Tyndale? in *The Tyndale Society Journal* No.38 Spring 2010 pp.10-24 for the identification of Hychyns with Tyndale.

[34] Edward Halle *The Union of the Two Noble Houses of Lancaster and York* 2nd edition of 1550 p. cxxvii (Scolar Press, Yorkshire 1970).

[35] Richard Rex New Light on Tyndale and Lollardy in *Reformation* Vol. 8 2003 p. 148ff for the suggestion of error in the bishop's register.

[36] W.R.Cooper, Ed. *The New Testament Translated by William Tyndale The Text of the Worms Edition of 1526 in Original Spelling* (The British Library, London 2000). *The New Testament : A Facsimile of the 1526 Edition* translated by William Tyndale with an introduction by David Daniell (Hendrickson, Peabody, Massachusetts 2008).

[37] David Daniell *William Tyndale A Biography* (Yale University Press, New Haven & London 1994). This is a major study of William Tyndale, particularly authoritative on his translations and theological writings, published to mark the quincentenary of Tyndale's birth. Professor Daniell is Chairman Emeritus of the Tyndale Society of which he was the founder (www.tyndale.org).

[38] For a useful selection of extracts from some of Tyndale's writings : David Daniell ed. *William Tyndale Selected Writings* (Carcanet Press, Manchester 2003). For a study of his theology : Ralph S. Werrell *The Theology of William Tyndale* (James Clarke & Co, Cambridge 2006) & *The Roots of William Tyndale's Theology* (James Clarke & Co, Cambridge 2013).

[39] David Daniell ed. *Tyndale's Old Testament: Being the Pentateuch of 1530, Joshua to 2 Chronicles of 1537, and Jonah.* A modern spelling edition. (Yale University Press, New Haven & London 1992).

[40] William Tyndale, Yet Once More To The Christian Reader in David Daniell Trans. *Tyndale's New Testament 1534* (New Haven and London : Yale University Press 1995 edition) pp. 13-16 for Tyndale on Joye.

[41] There is reference to Monmouth as Governor in De Smet (1950-54) see note 29. More easily accessible material on the role of Governor of the Merchant Adventurers can be found in Anne F. Sutton *The Mercery of London : Trade, Goods and People, 1130-1578*

(Aldershot : Ashgate 2005) with a reference to Monmouth (himself a member of the Drapers' Company) as Governor on p. 414. For Monmouth also see : Andrew Hope New Research on Humphrey Monmouth in *The Tyndale Society Journal* No.31 August 2006 pp. 28-34.

[42] John Foxe Ed. *The Whole Works of W. Tyndall, John Frith, and Doct. Barnes, three worthy Martyrs, and principall teachers of this Churche of England* (London : John Daye 1573) for the description of Tyndale at this time. David Daniell *William Tyndale A Biography* (New Haven & London : Yale University Press 1994) pp.316 & 331 for his comments on the 1534 translation.

[43] Andrew J. Brown *Robert Ferrar: Yorkshire Monk, Reformation Bishop, and Martyr in Wales* (London : Inscriptor Imprints 1997) & Andrew Hope in *ODNB* for further information about Constantine. TNA SP1/101/231 Thomas Poyntz to Henry VIII for details about the sending of Ferdinando to school

[44] John Foxe, *The Unabridged Acts and Monuments Online* or *TAMO* (1563 edition) (HRI Online Publications, Sheffield, 2011). Available from: http//www.johnfoxe.org [Accessed: 22.01.13].

[45] David Daniell *William Tyndale A Biography* (New Haven & London : Yale University Press 1994) Chapter 13 for discussion of Matthew's Bible. J.L. Chester *John Rogers* (London 1861) p. 25. David Daniell in *ODNB* for further information on Rogers.

[46] J.F. Mozley *William Tyndale* (London : SPCK 1937) p. 298 refers to a BCL gained in February 1533 according to Oxford Registers, but in J. Foster *Alumni Oxoniensis* Vol. III (Oxford 1892) there is an entry : 'Philips, Henry BCL 17/05/32-3'. Information on Brerewood and Underhill is from the various relevant university and ecclesiastical listings. The reference to Audley is from L&P XII Pt.1/764 & 835.

[47] J.F. Mozley *William Tyndale* (London : SPCK 1937) p. 298 for idea that this man was Maurice Semer, incumbent at East Morden which included a chapel at Charborough.

[48] P. Arblaster et al eds. *Tyndale's Testament* (Belgium : Brepols Publishers 2002) p. 12 for a photograph and full reference of the matriculation document. This book accompanied an exhibition on Tyndale at the Museum Plantin-Moretus, Antwerp, in 2002.

[49] For a fuller consideration of the plot see A Postscript : Who killed William Tyndale? (p.69).

[50] BL Cotton Galba Bx.6 August 1535 Thomas Poyntz to John Poyntz.

[51] William Tyndale. *The Obedience of a Christian Man* 1528 ed. and introd. David Daniell (London : Penguin Books 2000). I am grateful to Professor Daniell for comments on suggestions made in this section regarding the possible influence of *The Obedience...* on the thinking of Thomas Poyntz.

[52] In 1531 efforts had been made to persuade Tyndale to return to England. He refused, in the belief that the conservatives in the church would persuade the king to act against him once he was back. Stephen Vaughan to Henry VIII BL Cotton Galba B.x42 , to Thomas Cromwell TNA SP1/65 f178, to Henry VIII BL Add MSS 28583 f196 & to

Thomas Cromwell TNA SP1/65 ff271-273. Cromwell eventually told Vaughan that the king thought it better that Tyndale did not return and infect others with his views BL Cotton Galba B.x338 and Vaughan conveyed this message to Tyndale TNA SP1/66 f59.

[53] liefer = rather.

[54] David Daniell Trans. *Tyndale's New Testament* (New Haven and London : Yale University Press 1995) The Gospel of Saint John Chapter Eleven p. 151.

[55] L&P Vol.IX/498 August 1535 Cromwell's Remembrancer. TNA SP1/96 4th September 1535 Stephen Vaughan to Thomas Cromwell acknowledges two letters about Tyndale.

[56] BL Cotton Galba Bx.62 (Item 33) 22nd September 1535 Robert Flegge to Thomas Cromwell.

[57] TNA SP1/96/208 21st September 1535 John Poyntz to Thomas Cromwell.

[58] Fine on Jan Baers 1536 : Brussels, Archives generales du Royaume, Chambre de Comptes, nr.21.719 : translation in R. Demaus *William Tyndale : A Biography* (London : The Religious Tract Society 1871) revised edition ed. by R. Lovett 1886 p. 457. Poyntz is described as 'a prisoner who was accused of Lutheranism'.

[59] BL Cotton Galba Bx.81 Phillip's fears about the merchants were noted by Thomas Theobald in writing to Thomas Cranmer in the previous July.

[60] TNA SP1/102 March 1536 Mary Basset to Philippa Basset, reproduced in Byrne, Muriel St. Clare ed. *The Lisle Letters* (Chicago and London : University of Chicago Press 1981) Vol. 3 Item 588. It cannot be certain that this man was Henry Phillips but it seems very likely.

[61] TNA SP1/103 May 1536 Sir G. de Casale to Thomas Cromwell May 1536.

[62] Fragments of five letters survive addressed to individuals and towns in Germany between March and May 1536 in BL Cotton Vitellius B xxi/102. L&P X/535 from Vienna Archives March 1536 for Henry VIII to Charles V.

[63] TNA SP1/100/95-102. These letters are undated but seem to have been misplaced in TNA and L&P. The contents suggest winter 1536/7. There is a letter to each of his parents, to two brothers, to two brothers-in-law, and to Dr. Brerewood, Archdeacon of Barnstaple and Chancellor to the Bishop of Exeter. He mentioned having written to Dr. Underhill but this letter does not survive.

[64] TNA C65/147 April 1539 Act of Attainder of the Marquis of Exeter and others. TNA SP1/172/47-48 & 185-189 August & September 1542 Sir Thomas Seymour to Henry VIII for Phillips in Vienna.

[65] TNA SP1/101/231 Thomas Poyntz to Henry VIII.

[66] Henry Ellis *Original Letters Illustrative of English History* 1st Series Vol. II 1824-1846 (London : Dawsons of Pall Mall 1969) introd. by J.L.Kirby pp. 45/46 for Anne's intervention on behalf of Richard Harman.

[67] A Memorial from George Constantine to Thomas Lord Cromwell reproduced with an introduction by T. Amyot in *Archaeologia* (Society of Antiquaries) XXIII 1831 page 65.

[68] Acts of Court of the Mercers' Company 16th November 1536.

[69] J. Shakespeare & M. Dowling Religion and politics in mid-Tudor England through the eyes of an English Protestant woman : the recollections of Rose Hickman. *Bulletin of the Institute of Historical Research* lv pp. 94-102 May 1982 for Packington's dealing in books.

[70] Thomas Poyntz to Thomas Cromwell 1539 : NA SP1/156/105.

[71] L&P XIV/308 1539 Surrender of Holywell. F.G.Emmison *Tudor Secretary* (London : Longmans 1961) for further information on William Petre.

[72] Brian Buxton Ferdinando Poyntz : A Tudor Pupil at Burton in *Staffordshire History* Volume 40 Autumn 2004 for a fuller discussion of this matter, in particular the role of George Constantine and his links with Staffordshire. TNA SP1/101/231 Thomas Poyntz to Henry VIII.

[73] Statutes of the Realm Vol. 3 Chapter 25 Henry VIII 1541 for the Act of Naturalisation.

[74] TNA SP1/195/197 December 1544 Nicholas Wotton & Edward Carne to the Council.

[75] I am grateful to Dr. Paul Arblaster for information regarding concerns about heresy in Antwerp in 1544 which he described as "one of the busiest years of religious persecution in Antwerp in the first half of the century" (email 13th February 2004).

[76] TNA PROB 11/34/420 The will of Robert Tempest written in 1550/51 instructs that a bequest to Anna Poyntz was to be paid without any deduction of the money he had loaned her for her husband. Although no date is given for this loan it is possible that Robert had assisted towards extricating Thomas Poyntz from his dilemma despite the earlier problems between them over the removal of Ferdinando from school at Burton. Another possibility is that the reference is to money offered in 1535/6.

[77] TNA SP1/200/30 April 1545 Nicholas Wotton to the Council.

[78] I am grateful to Mr. Van Dijck Marten of the History Department, University of Antwerp, for consulting his 10,000 name database, derived from the fifteenth and sixteenth century archives in Brussels, in order to look for any reference to legal matters relating to Thomas Poyntz which might shed further light on these events. The result was negative.

[79] TNA C66/836 December 1551 Letters Patent of Edward VI.

[80] TNA E101/426/8 Privy Purse Accounts for Edward VI 3-5. P.N.Sil for Sir John Gates in *ODNB*.

[81] LMA CLC/L/GH/D/001/MS11571/005 4th April 1552 Grocers' Company Wardens' Accounts.

[82] TNA PROB 11/31/550 1547 Will of John Poyntz.

LMA DL/A/A/006/MS09531/012/002 Register of Bishop Edmund Bonner for presentation by Anne in 1554 to the living of North Ockendon when a vacancy arose through the deprivation of John Benson for marriage after the repeal of legislation allowing clerical marriage. Benson had been a witness to John Poyntz's will.

[83] TNA PROB 11/37/ 21 Will of Anne Poyntz 1554. The jewellery is described in great detail. Two pieces derived from her marriage with John Poyntz, a chain of gold had belonged to him and a goblet had a cover engraved with the arms of Sibley and Poyntz. I am grateful to Ms. Hazel Forsyth, Senior Curator of Post Medieval Collections at the Museum of London, for giving time to discuss these items. She considers that the quantity was probably less than might have been expected for a woman of Anne's status, partcularly as regards rings. Possibly items had been given away previously, and on this point it may be relevant that neither Anne's daughter Frances, nor her sister Elizabeth, are named as recipients in the will.

[84] TNA C142/133/134 Inquisition Post Mortem 1562 for details of lands at that point. LMA DL/A/A/006/MS09531/012/002 Register of Bishop Edmund Bonner & LMA DL/A/A/006/MS09531/013/001 Register of Edmund Grindal for presentations of priests.

[85] TNA E115/305/65 1556 Certificate of Residence for tax purposes addressed to officials in Tower Ward (Parish of St. Olave) London.

[86] ERO D/Dbe M18 Court Roll. TNA C1/1391/20 1553-1558 action by Jane Warren.

[87] LMA CLC/L/GH/D/001/MS11571/005 & 006 Grocers' Company Wardens' Accounts.

[88] Brett Usher Foxe in London 1550-1587 in John Foxe, *Acts and Monuments [...]. The Variorum Edition.* [online] (hriOnline, Sheffield 2004). Available at: http://www.hrionline.ac.uk/foxe/. [Accessed: 10.04.2005]. Brett Usher acknowledges a debt to Susan Wabuda's article Henry Bull, Miles Coverdale, and the making of Foxe's Book of Martyrs in *Studies in Church History Vol. 30* (Oxford 1993).

[89] BL Cotton Galba B.x60 1535 Thomas Poyntz to John Poyntz 1535.

[90] LMA P69/DUN2/B/011/MS02968/001 Churchwardens' Accounts.

[91] A. Townsend. *The Writings of John Bradford* Vols. I & II (Cambridge : The Parker Society 1848 & 1853). The quotation appears in Vol. I p. 36 and in Vol.II p.xxix.

[92] Townsend, A. *The Writings of John Bradford* Vol. II (Cambridge : The Parker Society 1853). The letter to Elsing from Bradford in prison appears on pp. 67-72.

[93] John Foxe, *Acts and Monuments [...]. The Variorum Edition.* [online] (hriOnline, Sheffield 2004). Available at: http://www.hrionline.ac.uk/foxe/. [Accessed: 07.02.2006] 1570 p.2008.

[94] The material about Thomas Sponer is from the following sources : LMA P69/DUN2/B/011/MS02968/001 Churchwarden's Accounts of St. Dunstan's in the West. LMA CLC/W/JB/044/MS03018/001Farringdon Without Precinct Inquest

Minutes & Presentments (St. Dunstan in the West). Minutes of Goldsmiths' Company Court at Goldsmiths' Hall. TNA E/179 Tax Records. TNA E150/310/2 1527 Inquisition Post Mortem on William Poyntz. TNA PROB 11/31/546 1547 Will of John Poyntz. TNA PROB 11/37/21 1554 Will of Anne Poyntz.

[95] The possibility that Elizabeth Sponer was a natural sister of John can be discounted by a careful reading of his will. When he does refer to a natural sister he gives her Christian name : 'my sister Margaret Barley'. He does the same with his brothers Thomas and Edmund. Another example of this use of the phrase 'my brother..' can be found in the will of Sir John Shaa TNA PROB 11/14/204 when he makes reference to William Poyntz, his brother-in-law.

[96] LMA P69/DUN2/A/001/MS10342 Burial Register of St. Dunstan's in the West. LMA P69/DUN2/B/011/MS02968/001 Churchwardens' Accounts.

[97] BL Harley 425 folios 10-12 Petition of Humphrey Monmouth to Thomas Wolsey in answer to Articles presented against him. In the Harley catalogue the group of papers of which this is one is described as : 'A book in folio containing more of the papers of Mr John Fox and bought of Mr Strype'.

[98] David Daniell *William Tyndale : A Biography* (New Haven & London : Yale University Press 1994) p. 369; J.F. Mozley *William Tyndale* (London : SPCK 1937) p. 319.

[99] J.A. Kingdon *Incidents in the life of Thomas Poyntz and Richard Grafton, two citizens and grocers of London, who suffered loss and incurred danger in common with Tyndal, Coverdale, and Rogers, in bringing out the Bible in the vulgar tongue* (London : Privately printed by Rixon & Arnold 1895).

[100] R. Demaus *William Tyndale : A Biography* (London : The Religious Tract Society 1871) revised edition ed. Lovett, R. 1886 p. 414.

[101] Christopher Anderson, C. *The Annals of the English Bible* (London : William Pickering 1845) pp. 522/5.

[102] The Will of Gabriel Poyntz TNA PROB 11/111/39 1606 included a bequest for the 'maintenance reparations and continuance of the monuments, tombs, vault and other remembrances that I have caused to be made in the north chapel of the church of North Ockendon'.

[103] C. Garrett *The Marian Exiles* (Cambridge : Cambridge University Press 1938 Reprint 1966) pp. 260 & 358.

[104] TNA PROB 11/50/303 1568 Will of Ralph Latham of North Ockendon.

[105] LMA CLC/GH/D/001/MS 11571/006 & 007 Grocers' Company Wardens' Accounts.

[106] Brian Dietz, ed. *The Port and Trade of Early Elizabethan London* (London Record Society 1972) 1568 Item 669. LMA CLC/L/GH/B/001/MS11588/001 Grocers' Company Court Minute Book 1556-1591 entries under 1568 & 1572.

[107] Robert Lemon, ed. *Calendar of State Papers Domestic Elizabeth 1581 – 1590*.

[108] LMA P69/DUN1/A/001/MS07857/001 Registers of St. Dunstan in the East.

[109] LMA CLC/GH/D/001/MS11571/007 Grocers' Company Wardens' Accounts for Richard Saltonstall in Mincing Lane.

[110] Edward Halle *The Union of the Two Noble Houses of Lancaster and York* 2nd edition of 1550 p. cxxvii (Scolar Press, Yorkshire 1970).

[111] Christopher Anderson *The Annals of the English Bible* (London : William Pickering 1845) p. 417.

[112] Robert Demaus *William Tyndale A Biography* (London : The Religious Tract Society 1871) revised edition ed. R.Lovett 1886 pp. 390/391.

[113] J.F. Mozley *William Tyndale* (London : SPCK 1937) pp. 300/301.

[114] David Daniell *William Tyndale A Biography* (New Haven & London : Yale University Press 1994) p. 368.

[115] Brian Moynahan *If God Spare My Life* (Little, Brown 2002) p. 339 ff.

[116] BL Cotton Galba Bx.6 August 1535 Thomas Poyntz to John Poyntz.

[117] BL Cotton Galba B.x.81 July 1535 Thomas Theobald to Thomas Cranmer.

[118] TNA C65/147 Attainder of the Marquess of Exeter and others.

[119] BL Cotton Galba B.x.81 July 1535 Thomas Theobald to Thomas Cranmer.

[120] Christopher Anderson *The Annals of the English Bible* (London : William Pickering 1845) p. 534ff. Robert Demaus *William Tyndale A Biography* (London : The Religious Tract Society 1871) revised edition ed. R.Lovett 1886 p. 400.

[121] J.F. Mozley *William Tyndale* (London : SPCK 1937) p. 306.

[122] J.F. Mozley *William Tyndale* (London : SPCK 1937) pp. 306/307.

[123] TNA PROB11/43/613 Will of Richard Phillips 1560.

[124] TNA SP1/100/95-96 Henry Phillips to his mother.

[125] TNA SP1/100/98 & TNA SP1/128/114 Henry Phillips to Thomas Brerewood.

[126] L&P 12/1 Items 764, 835 & 1106.

[127] Apart from the three letters already mentioned there was one each to his father, a brother, two brothers-in-law, John Hutton & Christopher Joy. BL Cotton Galba B.x.81 July 1535 Thomas Theobald to Thomas Cranmer.

[128] TNA SP1/143/181-2 1539 Richard Layton to Thomas Cromwell.

[129] TNA SP1/101/80-81 1536 Robert Faryngton to Thomas Cromwell.

[130] I am grateful to staff of Devon Record Office for searching lists of ordinations and institutions for any reference to Phillips. No such references were found.